UPCOUNTRY

Jeremiah Burrow

UPCOUNTRY

Robert Kimber

Down East Books
Camden, Maine

Copyright © 1991 by Robert Kimber
All rights reserved
Originally published in 1991 by Lyons & Burford Publishers
First paperback edition: 2005

ISBN 0-89272-681-4

Printed and bound at Versa Press, Inc., East Peoria, Illinois
3   2   1

Down East Books
Camden, Maine
A division of Down East Enterprise,
publishers of *Down East* magazine

Book orders: 800-685-7962
www.downeastbooks.com

Library of Congress Control Number: 2004117843

FOR GREG

ACKNOWLEDGEMENTS

With the exception of "Summer's Boomerang," all these essays were first published in periodicals, many of them in somewhat different form. I am grateful to the editors of those publications for printing these pieces and for their permission to reprint them here.

"Sheep in the Parlor," "A Slipping-Down Farm," "Living a Dog's Age," and "Machines, Accursed and Wondrous," first appeared in *Country Journal;* "The Black-Fly Baron of Western Maine," in *Maine Times;* "November on Route 150" and "Living on the Edge," in *Yankee Homes;* and "The End of the Road," in *Yankee.* All the others were written as "Letter from Upcountry" columns in *Down East,* and I owe a special word of thanks to Dale Kuhnert and Davis Thomas not only for offering me that regular space but also for their editorial support and counsel.

I want to acknowledge here, too, that the title for "A Slipping-Down Farm" was suggested by Anne Tyler's novel *A Slipping-Down Life.*

Preface to the Paperback Edition

I'm delighted to see this book back in print. That it is once again available I owe to the good offices of my friend Wes McNair and of Michael Steere at Down East Books. It was Wes who suggested to Michael the idea of reissuing *Upcountry*, and it was Michael who agreed to act on that suggestion. I'm grateful to them both.

I am perhaps fonder of this book than any writer ought to allow himself to be, not because I believe it occupies some high place in the literary pantheon beyond its modest reach but because it contains glimpses of the people and places, the work and the play, that have made my own and my family's life here in inland, rural Maine so rich and rewarding.

This book also reminds me of the pleasures of working during the 1980s with a number of first-rate editors: David Sleeper at Blair and Ketchum's *Country Journal*, Tom Rawls at the American edition of *Harrowsmith Country Life*, Jim Collins at *Yankee* and *Yankee Homes*.

It seems especially appropriate, too, that this reprint is appearing with Down East Books because nineteen of the twenty-nine essays in it I wrote as "Letter from Upcountry" columns for *Down East* magazine at the suggestion of Dale Kuhnert, who was then managing editor of *Down East* and is now its editor-in-chief.

As I noted in the preface of this book when it first appeared in 1991, I chose to write about the various topics here—dogs, doughnuts, skis, pickerel, snow, among others—primarily because I thought it would be fun to write about them. Now, as then, I can only hope that readers will have fun reading about them.

Robert Kimber
Spring 2005

Contents

Preface

This book marks an anniversary of sorts. The essays in this collection, though all written over the last eight years, celebrate the twenty years my wife and I have lived on our old farm in Temple, Maine. And though I wrote almost all of these essays with specific publications in mind, I had complete freedom in my choice of topics and how I would handle them. So the primary reason why you will find, among other things, pieces on sheep, dogs, Christmas trees, Mount Katahdin, and black flies here is that I thought it would be fun to write them.

A collection like this, generated mostly by whimsy and over several years, can't be accused of having an ulterior motive or an intentional theme that was planted in it right from the start. But now that these essays are gathered together, I see that there is an implicit *Apologia Pro Vita Sua* in them. Just about any one of them provides a partial answer to why, twenty years ago, Rita and I pulled up our Cambridge stakes and exchanged our work as university teachers of German and comparative literature for the precarious business of piecing together a living as part subsistence farmers, part writers, translators, and editors, in rural western Maine.

Just about any of them also provides a partial answer to the larger question we all keep asking ourselves and that only our closest friends dare to ask: "What are you doing here?"—a question that can be asked with the stress on the "you," the "doing," or the "here."

For what *I'm* doing here, I turn to Aldo Leopold, who has already said so much of what any of us needs to hear that I could quote him all day: "There are some who can live without wild things, and some who cannot," Leopold wrote in the foreword of *A Sand County Almanac.* "These essays are the delights and dilemmas of one who cannot." I don't think I can improve on that. The wild things take in, of course, not just the birds and beasts but also the lupine and the meadowsweet, the snowflakes, the sun coming up over the hills in the east and dropping over the hills in the west. I'm just among the some who cannot live without them.

As for what I'm *doing,* these pages should make that clear enough. I'm writing, getting the firewood in, helping out some with the garden, plowing the snow, beating back the brush, and—like any other sensible person—trying to find as much time as possible to fish, paddle, and roam the hills. When the occasional bemused visitor, ignorant of country ways, asks, "But what do you people find to do here? I should think you'd be bored to death," I hand him a typewriter, a shovel, a chain saw, and a fly rod, and I tell him, "When you're done with these, we'll go for a walk."

Why here? Because I have a special hankering for the kind of wild things native to this part of inland, upland, outback Maine. No lobster pots or lighthouses grow here. Maine's highest peaks, after Katahdin, rise just to the west of us. There are mountains to climb; woods to wander; numberless streams, rivers, ponds, and lakes to explore. I never tire of the view out our kitchen windows onto Spruce Mountain and Day Mountain.

The hills are steep; the soil is poor. You can log some of this country with difficulty and farm less of it with even more difficulty, so you wind up doing some of each. A couple of hours travel to the north takes you into Quebec. This is border territory in every sense, a place between French and English, a place where people live with one foot only tentatively testing the waters of mainstream America and the other still firmly planted in the ancient ways of piecing life together and making do. The cycle of the year still counts here. People cut next year's firewood while they're burning this year's. They sugar off in March, pick fiddleheads in May, plant on Memorial Day, and harvest on Labor Day.

But to tally up the things you love about a place does not explain why you love them, and finally you just throw up your hands and say, "Elective affinities," or "Gee, I don't know. I just like it here." If I need any excuse for being where I am, I guess that will have to do.

UPCOUNTRY

I would have a hard time accounting for why I have arranged these pieces in the sequence I have, and about all I can say is that I like the ebb and flow of seasons, subjects, and themes this arrangement yields. The sequence in no way reflects chronology, either in the order in which the pieces were written or in the times and events recorded in them. In a few cases, as in "Living a Dog's Age," the point in time is a present that is now several years in the past. I have tried to smooth the path back and forth between present and past, and I hope the reader will be able to travel it without too many bumps and jolts.

I want to thank everyone at Lyons & Burford who has had a part in the production of this book, and especially Nick Lyons, who has brought to this project his customary generosity, care, literary judgment, human kindness, and regard for the writer's metier.

The two most long-standing contributors to this book are, of course, my wife and son, Rita and Greg, and if I spent the rest of my days doing nothing but thanking them for the fun, work, and love we have shared in our twenty years of Temple time and the nineteen of Greg's lifetime, I still could not thank them enough.

Upcountry

Getting Lost

It's about three o'clock on a late winter afternoon. The air is soft and still and not too cold, and for the last couple of hours big feathery snowflakes have been sifting down out of a leaden gray sky. Over the ash pile, the compost heap, the chicken manure, the sawdust and splinters in the woodyard, the carpet of seed hulls under the bird feeder, over all the lees and dregs of daily life, they have laid their mantle of fluffy, unflecked purity.

I have been dutifully piling up words since seven-thirty this morning the way a logger does cordwood. But now the brain has run dry, and my feet are dancing restlessly under the desk. Like any old dog, I need my daily run. No matter what the weather, I have to get outside, snuff around in the underbrush, wag my tail, and bark up a few trees. Today, with the invitation of the new-fallen snow, the urge is irresistible.

Out past the garden, through the old sheep pasture, across Temple Stream on the ice, across the big hayfield on the other side, and up into the hills. My snowshoes leave regular stitches behind me in the new, white velvet. I stick out my tongue to catch the flakes, turn my face up to the sky to bask in the cool nips of this benevolent swarm.

The snowfall is not thick enough to cut off my view of the hills across the valley, but, seen in the open fields, it is a mass phenomenon nonetheless, like millions of fish in a school or thousands of geese rising from the water in a flock. In the woods, though, each flake seems differentiated, even to the naked eye. I can watch one parachute down to land on a hemlock branch, then another float all the way to the ground and settle on the toe of my snowshoe. Out here, I'm moved to suggest just one minor change in Portia's speech about the quality of mercy: it droppeth not as the gentle rain from heaven but as the gentle snow.

I zigzag up the steep hill through open hardwoods and past the south-facing ledges where snowmelt on sunny days freezes at night into ribbed, translucent pillars of ice. Under the canopies of small hemlock stands, there are only six or eight inches of snow on the ground compared to the two or three feet in the open, and I stop for a moment, thinking smugly what a snug little camp I could make here in the shelter of these trees.

The top of this ridge is not the smooth, domed hill the

topo map would suggest. Instead, it is folded and convoluted, with high plateaus here, granite outcroppings there, and small boggy flats that overflow in intermittent streams in the spring. It is an exquisite microcosm of western Maine hill country, one I never tire of walking, and one I feel I know better than the back of my hand.

Today's outbound ramble ends in a thick stand of fir with a tiny marshy meadow at its center, a patch of flawless, trackless white that I come to the edge of but do not walk on, preferring to leave this page blank for a more delicate scribe. The afternoon is wearing on; the light is fading; the air is cooler. The snow is falling faster, smaller, thicker. Lacy and ornamental only half an hour ago, it is now dense and foglike, interfering with vision, not enhancing it.

It's time to head for the kitchen stove. I push my way out of the thick black growth and don't retrace the long, looping trail that brought me here but take a straight line across the ridge, intending to pick up my own tracks just where they come up onto the top of the hill.

Fifteen minutes later I have not picked up my tracks, nor am I on the hardwood slope where I know they are. An old familiar feeling is creeping over me, but it is not one that repeated experience has made any more comfortable or enjoyable. I'm screwed up, turned around, in a word, lost. The snowfall that lured me out here has conspired with the fading light to play tricks on me. In full daylight and with no snow, I would probably recognize as old friends every tree and snow-shrouded rock I'm looking at right now. But in this combined whiteout/grayout, even my own feet look like alien beings.

"Lost," of course, is not quite the right word to describe my predicament. I know that I'm in a dinky triangular patch of woodland bordered on two sides by dirt roads and by Temple Stream on the third side, that Temple Stream lies due west of me, that I'm about half a mile from my own house, and that even if I chose the worst possible direction to walk in, a mile's travel would bring me out.

But knowing all that at dusk on a dark, snowy day is not too helpful because I don't have enough daylight left to bushwhack a mile. I have only enough daylight left to reach my back field if I travel due west, right on the money. And I haven't a clue where west is. I've landed in a rolling little patch of terrain where I can't tell from the lay of the land which way is down into the valley, and because of the snow, I can't see far enough to make an educated guess. I may be just confused rather than lost, but for my purposes right now, with darkness coming on, confused is as good as lost.

The panic that sets in at this point is more social than physical in origin. The discomfort of a night in the woods would be as nothing compared to the humiliation. There may be some excuse for getting lost in the wilds of northern Quebec. But, quite literally, in your own backyard? I hope my family will have the good grace to let me expire out here before they call in a search-and-rescue team. Death I could endure, but the disgrace of the next day's news story, never. "Temple Man, Believed Lost, Found Bivouacked Two Hundred Yards from His Own Back Door."

But even as this fantasy flits through my mind, I remember the compass that's always in my jacket pocket, usually unneeded and half-forgotten but oh, so nice to have at a moment like this. Aha, so west is *that* way. I never would have guessed. Ten minutes later I hit the little trickle of a stream that swings off to the north, skirts the hemlock-covered bluff above my back field, and then heads west again into Temple Stream.

Being lost, whether for five minutes or half an hour or half a day, is unsettling at the time but, in retrospect, always a bracing corrective. So I think I know this wooded hillside like the back of my hand? So I think the snow is falling for my delectation? Or in a deliberate, diabolical effort to bamboozle me? Wrong, wrong, and wrong again. I have only a passing acquaintance with these woods, and the snow is falling neither to delight nor blind me. It is simply falling, faintly falling upon all the living and the dead. And as I push through it, heading across the field and stream toward the halo of light on my back porch, I find that both right and comforting. It is the snow, finally, that is in charge out here, not I.

Sheep in the Parlor

Sheep came into our lives the way just about every other creature on our place has come: unplanned, unpremeditated, flung our way, so to speak, by the forces of benign rural chaos. It was midsummer, our second on the tumbledown, overgrown old farm we had bought in western Maine. Rita was working in the garden; I was peeling split and curled clapboards off the front of the house in plain view of all who passed on the road. Among the passersby was our neighbor Leo Rioux, who at the time was still running a small dairy farm two miles up the intervale. His truck screeched to a halt, the gears complaining bitterly as he shifted into reverse and rumbled into the driveway tail-end first.

The body of the truck was filled with assorted forlorn livestock.

"What this place needs," Leo said as he leapt down from the cab, "is a couple of sheep."

There were exactly two sheep on the truck. One was a black-faced, black-legged, gray-muzzled, round-bellied, bony-hipped old ewe that stood braced squarely on all four feet and looked me straight in the eye, her head tilted pugnaciously to one side. "Let it be understood right now," she said, "before negotiations go a step further, that this lady takes guff from nobody."

Her companion was an immense wool ball, dirty white all over. He was so round and woolly that it was hard to locate his feet and head, much less his eyes, ears, and mouth. But even though I had trouble telling one end of him from the other, I did get the impression that he was young and good-natured and would be happy to roll around our place like a huge fleecy bowling ball, knocking down anything in his path.

"I can give you an awful good trade on 'em," Leo said. A lean, dark-haired man, Leo spoke and moved with a quick authority that was hard to resist. He was already unloading the sheep before I had said a word.

"How much?" I managed to blurt out.

"Twenty-five for the pair."

Rita had heard Leo's truck arrive and had come up from the garden to join us. She falls for anything fuzzy and four-footed, and I could see a familiar, almost narcotic glaze form over her eyes. If she had said anything, it would have been, "Aren't they dear?"

"What am I gonna do with sheep, Leo?" I said. "I don't

have any fencing. I don't have a shed. I don't know anything about sheep."

"You can send me a check," he said, and climbed back into his truck.

As he turned onto the main road, I took a closer look at the old ewe. The reason she had looked at me with her head tilted to one side was that she was blind in one eye.

"Hey, Leo," I shouted.

But he was already gone, his hand waving out the window of his truck.

And, as Rita said later, if she's healthy, so what? The lack of one eye didn't slow the Old Lady down at all. I hate to think what she might have accomplished if she'd had two.

Because we had no fencing, I thought it would be clever to tether the Old Lady. Not only would that keep her under control (along with, presumably, her son, whom we christened the Oaf), but it would also enable us to use our new sheep to battle brush and grass. The sheep would gobble up everything within the radius of the Old Lady's tether; then I would move the stake. I could already imagine our neglected old farm gradually being restored to trimmed beauty, one overlapping circle after another.

But the Old Lady had told me she would take no guff, and she had meant it. She pulled up the tether stake and went where she pleased. When I used a stronger stake and drove it deeper into the ground, she tangled both herself and the Oaf in the rope so thoroughly that the struggles of each to get loose would topple the other. A hideous bleating and blatting followed. When I ran to their rescue, the Old Lady always looked on the verge of strangulation, a purplish tongue lolling from her mouth. Purple, of course, was the natural color of her tongue, but I didn't know that then, and she knew I didn't know it. She was not above cheap histrionics when they served her purpose, and her purpose was to have the run of the place. After two or three melodramas at the stake, she got it.

One of the most ancient and persistent misconceptions humankind is given to is that sheep are stupid. The longevity of that delusion attests not so much to the witlessness of sheep as it does to our narrow, self-serving ideas of intelligence. We tend to think animals that learn to do what we want them to do, and like us into the bargain, are smart. Sheep are ineducable and don't give a damn about us; therefore, we conclude, they are stupid. Granted, they are flock animals and prefer to rush into disaster as a mob rather than seek safety as individuals. But we humans are hardly immune to that kind of behavior ourselves.

I suppose it is true that sheep are not particularly skilled at abstract reasoning, but then they are rarely called on to solve abstract problems; and whatever they may lack in rational powers they make up for in character. Or such has been our limited experience of them. We have never kept many sheep, our flock ranging from a minimum of three to a maximum of sixteen. Then, too, this odd little line we have developed by sheer accident may be atypical. The Old Lady, the mother of them all, clearly had a strong dose of Suffolk in her. The mate we found to keep her company after the Oaf went into the freezer was a brown, rangy, aquiline-nosed, well-behorned ram who was covered with something closer to deer hair than to wool. Indeed, he looked something like a cross between a deer, a goat, and a sheep. The neighbor from whom we got him advised us that his lineage was Barbados, more or less. We called him Rambaud.

The following spring the Old Lady produced twins, as she would right up to the spring she quite literally turned up her toes and died. With sheep strength up to four, the Old Lady decided she would make a bid for total control over the place. The summer before, with only the Oaf as her ally, she had been content to win her freedom to roam the farm at will. But now, backed by an athletic mate and two daughters who had inherited her brains and his brawn, she decided it was time to move out of the old chicken coop I had converted to a sheep shed and take over the house.

Her campaign started on the porch. When it was time for the midday siesta and cud chewing, the Old Lady and her crew would head for the back porch and rattle up the steps onto the shaded deck. Santa's eight tiny reindeer never made such a clatter.

If I was at my desk, I would race outside yelling, "Scram! Beat it!" and herd my visitors off. But they would come back, and the scene would be repeated. If we were away for a couple of hours we would come home to find a woolly welcoming committee waiting for us on the porch. Judging by the amount of manure on the deck, they had moved in the minute they had seen the car pull out of the drive.

"I don't think they'll ever learn," Rita said.

"Of course they will," I'd say, shoveling and sweeping the boards clean. "If I keep booting them off this porch eight or nine times a day, they'll get the point sooner or later. No animal is that stupid."

After several weeks it began to dawn on me that in this particular duel of wits, I was not faring well. The sheep were having a lovely time. What was it to them if they were kicked off a porch several times a day? The lambs, Marion and Muriel, thought the porch game particularly good fun. They enjoyed looking in the kitchen window to see what the people were up to, and if they saw me coming, they would tip off their parents. "Here he comes!" they'd say, and bound off the porch only to run back up again while I was shoving Rambaud and the Old Lady off.

The lesson finally sank in when, after what may well have been the 437th encounter, I overheard Rambaud say to the Old Lady, "I don't think he'll ever learn."

"Of course he will," the Old Lady said. "If we just persist he'll get the point sooner or later. No animal is that stupid."

The next day I erected a fence around the porch. It was a hasty, makeshift job, and it irritated me no end that I had to climb over a fence to get onto my own porch. But it did keep the sheep off. The usual procedure, I knew, was to fence the sheep in, not the shepherd. But I was pushing hard to make more of our house livable for the next winter, and I didn't want to take time out to fence in a sheep pasture.

The sheep took great interest in the renovation project. As I jacked the house up and tore out rotting sills, they would hang around and kibitz.

"If I were you, I'd put in another prop before I yanked that section out."

"There's dry rot in the bottom two feet of that corner post. Better splice in a new piece."

They were usually right, but that hardly made their advice welcome. The Old Lady was especially pushy, and more than once I had to postpone swinging an axe or hammer because, chewing away like a teenager with a mouthful of gum, she would stick her head between the tool and its target.

In an old farmhouse, one step leads to another. If you replace a sill, you'll be forced to remove some weathered, shattered siding beneath which you'll find shaky, splintered sheathing haphazardly tacked to randomly spaced studs. Faced with such prospects, folks even less compulsive than I are moved to rip out everything but the post-and-beam framing and start over again. So in one frenzied afternoon, I tore out the south and east walls of what had been the parlor. Because we were already late for supper with some friends, I cleaned up hastily, and we set off.

When we came home about nine o'clock, the sheep were comfortably settled in the parlor, the Old Lady with her knitting, Rambaud with his paper, the kids sprawled on the floor playing Go Fish. The two-foot leap into the wide-open building had been no obstacle. The Old Lady allowed that the room was pleasant enough but seemed rather bare of furnishings.

Over the next couple of days, the sheep kept leaping into the house to check up on my progress, ask endless questions, and stick their curious noses into every phase of the operation. Uppermost in their minds, though, was when the place would be ready for them to move in permanently. So it came as something of a shock to them when the walls went up without a ramp and a sheep door. They were miffed, and they were even more miffed when, after I had finished working on the house for that summer, I finally got around to fencing them into the field where I thought they should stay.

"Now," I thought, "I've done it right. My troubles are over." But as every neophyte shepherd soon learns, there is something that doesn't love a fence, and that something is a sheep. The Old Lady may have had Suffolk blood in her, but she must have had a strong streak of Houdini as well. In the spring and summer, when the pasturage was lush and plentiful, she was content to stay on her side of the fence. Our tiny flock had the run of a cleared pasture plus another four or five acres of mixed brush, grass, and alders beyond it. Two sides of this area were blocked off by my new fence; Temple Stream formed a barricade on the third side; and there were alders and a bogan, or marshy backwater, on the fourth.

All went well until sometime in September, when the choice food on the sheep's range had been eaten up and when the shortening days and frosty nights told them that the days of milk and honey were just about over. The grass on our side of the fence looked greener (it actually was greener). Memories of the good old days of grazing around the house and garden came alive (when it comes to remembering good eating places, sheep put elephants to shame). The Old Lady's ingenuity and spirit were roused.

Was there a place where the fence was not stretched piano-string tight? She would burrow under it. Was one of the twelve-inch gaps in the mesh more like thirteen or fourteen inches? She would stick her head through and lean and push until she had a hole large enough to wriggle through. In later years, when the flock was larger and the fence even weaker, she organized her troops into a phalanx and smashed through with brute force. If I had patrolled the fence carefully and reinforced it, she would bide her time, waiting until the ice in the bogan had thickened enough to let her cross. Then she would lead her band of guerillas onto one neighbor's lawn, into another neighbor's strawberry fields. Smart she was, a smart old sheep. And her intelligence runs in the family. Her daughters, Marion and Muriel, are still with us; and they are every bit as clever as their mother was. Chain them, put them in a trunk, sink them in a pond, and they'll pop to the surface again inside of a minute.

In *The Sheep Book*, Ronald Parker introduces his system for evaluating ewes with these wise words: "If your flock is small, you may have some favorites that you are reluctant to send off for slaughter. At the very least you may not be very objective about culling if you have an emotional attachment to some of the animals. To prevent this pitfall you can rank your ewes numerically." Parker then suggests assigning percentage points for desirable characteristics: profligacy, 30; lamb raising, 30; health, 10; fleece, 10; and genetics, 20. You then set a minimum acceptable score, say 70 or 75 percent, and cull any ewes that fall below it. Each shepherd can adapt this system to his or her own needs. My own scale goes something like this: On the plus side are profligacy, 25; lamb raising, 25; health, 35; omnivorousness, 5; taste of lambs produced, 10. On the negative side, obstinacy, −25; escape and evasion, −25; intelligence, −25; meddlesomeness, −10;

ability to make a sentimental fool of the shepherd, −15. I then add the plus and minus percentages together, and any ewe who falls between 20 and −20 percent I keep. The Old Lady and her daughters all scored a perfect zero.

If your flock is small, in other words, your supposedly stupid sheep may well make a dummy of you. Mine have been highly successful at that, running roughshod over whatever minimal business instincts I have, though I am thankful that I can say we don't lose any money on our sheep. We have ample pasturage for our small flock and more than enough hay for winter feed. Our animals have been remarkably healthy and hardy for what I suspect is a combination of reasons: uncrowded living conditions, happily haphazard crossbreeding, and complete freedom of expression. Costs for medical supplies and veterinary services are low, and grain cost is our only real outlay.

But if sheep are not a serious business proposition, why keep them at all? Well, if you have a taste for lamb and if you ever have a chance to eat lamb chops at my house, you'll know one good reason. The difference between the lamb we raise and what we can buy in the store is the difference betwen ambrosia and a Big Mac.

And then there are the lambs in their first few weeks and months, those lanky-legged, airplane-eared little creatures who bounce into the air as though propelled by four pogo sticks. There is perhaps no other young animal that touches us more with the sweetness, brightness, and glee of new life. And then, of course, in the depths of winter when Rita and I are feeling a little dull, it's nice to know that we can always invite Marion and Muriel up to the parlor for a little tea and intelligent conversation.

No Night Life

Country towns have no night life. I like that. I like to find a village asleep if I happen to roll into it any time after nine P.M. And I roll into a lot of small towns at that hour and later. That's an inevitable condition of the trout fisherman's life. Say I drive up to the South Branch of the Dead River or somewhere north of The Forks for an afternoon and evening's fishing. I will, without fail, stay on the water until it is much too dark to see. It's too dark to tie on a new fly, too dark to see the water, too dark to see the trees in which I hang up my fly and therefore have to tie on a new fly that it is too dark to see. A headlamp would solve part of my problem, and one of these years—at the promptings of that voice in me that always says "Just one more cast, just one more cast"—I may take a headlamp along. But the reason I probably don't take one with me now is that another voice urges obedience to the fading sun and the deepening shadows, and when they say it's time to quit, I quit.

So by the time I wallow out of the water and get back to the car, it's well after nine o'clock. Allow whatever travel time it takes to get to Rangeley or Bingham or wherever, and it's a cinch the place will not be booming. If you're hungry, you're out of luck. The restaurants, if there are any, are closed. The stores harbor only the dim illumination of their night lights and Coors signs. You may find a mom-and-pop store still open where you can pick up a Table Talk apple pie or a Devil Dog. Otherwise, it's back to the peanuts and apricots left over in your pack.

A rare car trundles slowly down the main, and just about only, street. Three kids on bikes whoosh silently by like earthbound bats. Some slightly older kids, male and female, squeak and squawk, running away from each other, running back together, bobbing, weaving, punching, pulling, squeezing, wrestling, tickling, slathering for each other's flesh but not quite knowing how to go about it in earnest, or whether they dare to.

In Stratton, Cathy's Place is officially closed, but you may be able to kid and cajole a sandwich out of the crew cleaning up in the kitchen. The waitresses are sitting at the tables having a last smoke; the few customers still left have empty coffee cups or beer glasses in front of them and their NAPA caps pushed back on their heads. Business is over for today. You can't quite tell who is guest and who is help. This motel dining room isn't a commercial operation anymore. It's a place where a few folks have finished their day and are shooting the breeze together until somebody decides it's time to head home to bed.

You cannot buy gas. In larger towns downriver, like Skowhegan and Farmington, you can. They have been infiltrated by Seven-Eleven and Cumberland Farms and, worse yet, that most flagrant of the stay-up-all-night food-and-fuel hucksters, the Irving Big Stop. A Boeing 707 could land on that vast tarmac bathed in eye-splitting white light.

But in the small river towns and nonriver towns up-country no gas flows. Just how tightly shut down the pumps can be I discovered a few years ago after a pad-dling companion and I finished an Allagash trip late in the afternoon. We were in Allagash Village. Our car was in Greenville. We had two options: We could camp over-night in the village and have Folsom's Air Service pick us up in the morning. Or we could find somebody in Alla-gash to drive us back to Greenville that night. I love camp-ing in the bush, but I hate camping in or near towns, so we started looking for a driver, and we were lucky enough to find that broad-beamed and kindly Allagash guide, Wil-mer Hafford.

After setting off in Wilmer's huge gas-guzzling van at six or six-thirty, we found the fuel gauge tilting toward low about the time we turned west off the Turnpike at Howland. We allowed as we would stop at the first gas station we saw.

I think our first stop was in or near LaGrange. I really don't remember the location, but I do remember the mute passivity of two gas pumps and a dark little storefront that would not come to life for any amount of knocking, even though the owners were clearly at home upstairs watching TV. They were absolutely right not to respond. Anybody driving around after dark shouldn't be encouraged.

"Well," Wilmer said, "we'll try it in Milo."

Milo is bigger, but as far as gas was concerned, it was no better. And the hour was later still, ten o'clock, ten-thirty maybe.

"Well," Wilmer said, "we'll try it in Dover."

How many more towns would we be able to reach on an empty gas tank? I don't like camping on roadsides much more than I like camping in town, but I was beginning to brace myself for it, particularly when the gas pumps of Dover-Foxcroft greeted us with the same lack of enthusiasm as their cousins in Milo and LaGrange had.

But before Wilmer's ever-optimistic nature could say, "Well, we'll try it in Guilford" or Abbot Village or Monson, I spotted a police car slowly cruising the streets, and I jumped out of the van to flag it down.

"Is there any way we can get a tankful of gas at this hour?"

There was. Because it would not do for the police cars ever to run dry, the town had a contract with a local station. The duty cruiser had the key and could fuel up at any time. We pumped our gas; the officer collected the proper amount of money and left it on the owner's desk in the station.

I've always liked Dover-Foxcroft, and that considerate policeman made me like it even more. We got to Greenville and, after two more hours driving, home to our beds in Temple. Wilmer got home to Allagash. If things had gone strictly by the rules, we all would have slept in the van or by the roadside, for the rules are that in country towns you are forbidden to buy gas after eight P.M. The rules are that you stop and rest when it gets dark. You don't keep running all night on fumes, hot air, adrenalin, and nerves. In the country, day is day and night is night; and if you insist on buying gas at midnight, that's a matter for the police.

Now I always make sure I have plenty of gas when I go fishing so that I can revel in the lack of night life when I roll into a small town. I may even park on the main drag, get out of the car, and bask in that lack. The few street-lights and what little activity there is cannot push back the night; and the town's single main street, overarched by darkness and stars, is awash in coolness and quiet. If you walk to one end or the other of that street, you are back in the country again with the silhouettes of the hills black against the sky and the peepings, croakings, and rustlings of nocturnal creatures around you. Where there is no night life, the real life of the night can flood in on all your senses. The sky, the forest, and, where there is one, the river—the Kennebec, the Piscataquis, the Sandy, the Car-rabassett—will reassert their hold over a small town, reminding us that it is we who are beholden to them, not they who are beholden to us.

Trash Wood

The man who taught me most of what I know about firewood (and a number of other things as well) wouldn't settle for anything but the best. He and I spent a good part of each summer cutting the twenty-odd cords of firewood needed every year to feed the dozen heater stoves and the kitchen range in my father's hunting and fishing camp in western Maine. Don started washing dishes in a lumber camp at age twelve, and he had spent most of his adult life since then in the bush as a woodcutter, river rat, guide, game warden. He always wanted plenty of "biscuit wood" on hand, bone-dry white birch that would bring the oven up to 450 degrees in a matter of minutes. And for those windy January days at twenty below he believed in solid junks of rock maple seasoned for two years. His standards were infectious, and for many years I too would sniff disdainfully at any woodpile that was not made up of clean mixed hardwoods.

My retreat from that kind of purism began when I saw my wife's country cousins in Switzerland using twigs, prunings from the cherry trees, and just about any other ragtag scrap of wood to cook with and to fuel the tile stove in the living room, a great alp of a stove with ledges and pinnacles on which cats and humans could sprawl to soak up the heat radiating from that benign monster. Outside, next to the barn, was a roofed bin with lattice walls, and whoever found any stray piece of wood anywhere on his or her wanderings on the farm tossed that wood into the bin, a system that kept the farm tidy as only Swiss farms can be, and also provided an unending supply of fuel.

Granted, winters on the shores of Lake Constance are mildness personified compared to January in Maine, and when the thermometer drops well below zero at night and doesn't climb much above it during the day, I don't want to be fooling around with any twigs and scraps either. But for those long weeks in the spring and fall when the weather in northern New England is not all that different from a Thurgau winter (damp, cool, with temperatures lingering around the freezing point) I find I'm using more and more trash wood, either mixing it in with a few sticks of good stuff or burning it alone if the weather is mild enough.

The benefits are substantial. First is economy. For every stove-load of trash wood I burn, I don't burn some of that nice, clean hardwood that takes me time to cut, split, haul, and pile. If you buy your firewood, using trash wood can save you money. If you cut your own wood, it can save you time. And time, I have been told, is money. The second benefit is beauty and order. My place is still a long way from looking like a Swiss farm, but it's a lot neater than it was before I developed my mania for trash wood. I hitch a trailer onto the back of my Ford tractor and then go out on patrol, picking up all the dead branches that the wind has knocked out of the trees near the house and outbuildings, sawing up all the dead elms and demolished chicken coops the floods have washed down the stream and left stranded in my pastures. I fell and saw up any standing deadwood in sight.

I am not at all fussy about species. Willow, poplar, anything will do, even if all the books say it is the world's worst firewood. In the woods, I zip the limbs off fir blow-downs and haul the trunks home. The ideal trash wood ranges in size from sticks that can be broken up with your hands and feet to stuff four or five inches in diameter—in other words, stuff that requires only a swipe with the chain saw but no splitting. It should also be close to home. The whole point is to get quick fuel that does not cost you hauling and splitting time. Another time saver is not to pile it; and since a lot of trash wood is gangly and twisty, it's almost impossible to pile anyhow. Taking my clue from the Thurgau farmers, I just dump my loads of trash wood helter-skelter under a shed roof and yank it out as needed.

The third benefit is feeling smug for turning something to use that is ordinarily either left to rot or burned in great brush piles in the spring. On those rare occasions when I cut brush these days, I throw any stick of alder that's as big around as my wrist onto the trailer. When the lilacs that bloom in my dooryard get a little too dense, I thin them and saw the thinnings to stove length. No stick is too ridiculous or too sublime to be fed into the firebox. Using trash wood is a small-scale biomass operation, and once you start poking around for extra Btus in unlikely places, new possibilities will keep turning up. After I peeled some cedar fence posts, for example, I found I could take the strips of stringy bark, roll them up into a ball, and stuff them in the stove, where they made superb kindling. Then this last fall, as I was merrily cutting down some good clean hardwoods, I realized that there were several red oak tops strewn around me in the woods. How old they were I can't say, but I know no one has cut in that part of my woodlot in all the years I've been on this place. Just for curiosity, I cut into those huge tops and found, underneath a punky layer that was perhaps half an inch thick, a gold mine of solid red oak. Talk about feeling smug.

But smugness—enjoyable as it may be in the short run—is not a state of the soul I have much use for; and even as I was congratulating myself for making all this otherwise waste stuff serve my purposes, I was also beginning to suspect that the best thing about my trash-wood retrieval system was its inefficiency. A guy with a chain saw and a dinky little farm trailer isn't going to make too much of a dent on the deadwood in a hundred-acre wood-lot. But what if I could develop some clever and economical machine that would harvest *all* my trash wood, a big vacuum cleaner, maybe, that homed in on dead wood only and would suck my woods clean of every last snag, blow-down, and fallen twig? Pretty soon I'd have more trash wood than I could use, and I'd start selling it. I'd also start using phrases like "maximization of resource potential" and "economies of scale," most of which, when translated, seem to mean, "Let's squeeze poor old Mother Nature for the last nickel she can give us." I'd be well on my way to becoming a hyper-biomass engineer. The forest floor on my place would be cleaner than my kitchen floor. There'd be no den trees left, no standing deadwood to host the insects that feed the woodpeckers, no fallen tree trunks rotting and breaking down into soil. The fuel needed for that great, cyclic slow burn of decay and teeming regeneration would not be there.

The point is embarrassingly simple: In nature, there is no trash; and "trash wood" is a contradiction in terms, one that could occur only to an industrialized man like me who places different market values on different kinds of wood. In pre-biomass days, all the slash left over from cutting operations was "trash," too. It had no immediate dollar value. It was left to rot; and as it rotted, it helped the soil retain moisture, shaded it from the sun, returned nutrients to it, protected the microorganisms in it. In the dollar economy, it was worthless; but in nature's economy, it was a valuable resource. If we rob nature of slash and trash wood to profit from them ourselves, we may be letting ourselves in for another technological fix that will leave wrecked forests in its wake.

I'm not in any danger on my place. My technology is too primitive; and my biomass operation will never harvest more than a tiny fraction of all the dead and dying wood out there. So I'll be making a virtue of my technological insufficiency. In the meantime, I hope the folks who have the technological capability to turn every last twig of fir and needle of spruce into biomass fuel won't.

Backyard Canoeing

W hen the dense, humming heat of midsummer comes to western Maine and sets the mountains afloat in a purple haze, I find myself most given to backyard canoe trips. A backyard canoe trip is not by necessity an institution of July and August any more than a backyard cookout or a backyard beer sipped in tranquility is. But there is a certain propriety, a certain rightness, about the beer, the cookout, and the backyard canoe trip at this time of year.

The sun is a red ball in the evening sky; the cold bottle sweats and drips profusely in your hand, just as you sweated and dripped a few hours earlier when you put in a few new fence posts in the garden. The lamb-chop-scented smoke from the coals rises lazily in the soft, damp air. It's time to lie back on the grass and, if you're in a canoe, time to lie back in it. The days of those heroic, or at least semi-heroic, canoe trips that Maine is justly famous for are past for this year, those fifty- or sixty- or eighty-mile runs through country that is far from being wilderness any more but that can still afford you the illusion of wilderness. If you try the St. John this month, you'll probably walk more than you'll paddle; and most of the rivers that run swollen and swift in April and May, supplying canoe folk with their whitewater day trips in the spring, are mere trickles now. Some of them, like the Carrabassett and the Upper Sandy in my part of the state, are so low that you have trouble getting your feet wet in them, much less floating a canoe. The spring freshets and the rush of energy and adrenalin they inspire have ebbed; and the nip of fall in the air that will set us scrambling again to do those things we have not done this summer is still a few weeks away. This is the time of year to wallow slothfully and enjoy every minute of it, to take lazy float trips on the big, flatwater sections of the rivers, to poke around in the bogs and ponds near home.

The backyard canoe trip is really not a "trip" at all. It is instead an outing, an excursion; it remains local and domestic. You don't break into new territory so much as you get to know better what you already know. Trips call for more or less mighty preparations, for gathering of gear, arranging of logistics, a lengthy drive to the start, and a lengthy drive home from the finish. The backyard canoe outing calls, at most, for a lunch, an extra shirt, and your raingear tossed into a daypack. You don't need eight or ten topo maps. You just take out the DeLorme atlas and pick out any body of water within half an hour to an hour's drive from home; maybe it's one you've been on a dozen times already; or maybe it's one you've driven by or walked to but never paddled on before.

The big trip or expedition is like a courtship: new, exciting, heady, unpredictable, eye-opening, horizon-expanding. The pleasures of the backyard outing are more like those of marriage: the deepening appreciation for the familiar; the total relaxation; the registering of subtle changes that the loving, knowing eye is keen enough to perceive; the discoveries you keep making when it would seem there is nothing left to discover. It seems no accident to me that these little outings in the canoe have become one of Rita's and my favorite ways to spend a summer day together, sometimes with others, sometimes by ourselves.

Flagstaff Lake in northern Franklin County is one of the places we have gone to so often that it seems as familiar to me as our kitchen table and as much a part of what I call home. Whenever we have summer visitors who are here long enough to fit in a day outing or two comfortably, I always like to take them there. The lake is about fifteen miles long, and the huge, lovely mass of the Bigelow range extends along the whole length of its south shore. There aren't many places I know that can provide such an instant and spectacular answer to the question: "What is it you like so much about living in backcountry Maine?"

The wind can blow up something fierce on Flagstaff, so it's important to pick a wind-still, glassy-water day to go there because the ideal backyard canoe trip does not permit of hard work. And because Flagstaff is so expansive, it's good to have at least one other canoe crew along to help inhabit the landscape, and for the party to include some kids and dogs to bounce around in all that wide-open space.

We drive up through New Portland, through the open fields in Lexington, where you can see all of Mount Abraham stretched out for you in the west, then past the abandoned general store in Highland Plantation. At the little beach at the southwesterly toe of the lake we put the canoes in; and as we paddle out to the rocky ledges along the western shore, West Peak and Avery Peak on Bigelow seem to rise higher and higher against the blue of the sky.

The ledges, worn smooth by time, wind, and water, invite us to dive off them for a swim, stretch out on them and bake like lizards in the sun, eat a sandwich, drink a beer, and feel mellow beyond all words. I've never spotted any fossils on these rocks—no fish skeletons or dinosaur tracks—but with the summer sun inducing such delectable torpor, I can imagine never moving again and becoming a contented fossil myself, the image of indolence cast in stone for the ages.

But there is only so much fossilizing that kids and dogs can endure, and we are soon back in the boats again, paddles dipping and feathering languidly, the droplets that fall from the blades scattering like mercury on the mirror surface of the water. On the north shore opposite our rocky point and about a mile and a half away is a sand beach with such a flat slope to it that our canoes run aground six feet from shore, and we have to climb out to beach them. For reasons I don't understand but nontheless accept, dogs, kids, and adults all love running up and down a beach in six to eight inches of water, perhaps because there is no easier or more innocent way to make a big splash. But it is tiring, and the dogs are soon wading chin deep to cool off and lap water; the people are flopping full length, gawking at Bigelow's grandeur, and I am congratulating myself—maybe out loud, maybe silently—for living in a place where I have all this in my backyard.

All this and more, of course. Because Flagstaff is just one of a small million destinations for a backyard canoe trip. We could just as well have put in at Solon on the Kennebec, puzzled over the Abenaki petroglyphs on the shale ledge there, floated down the back channel around Gray Island, loafed and botanized on Indian and Fowl Meadow islands, and waded through the stands of shoulder- and head-high ostrich ferns there. Or we could have paddled up the Dead River in Leeds and into Androscoggin Lake where the beach on Norris Island is of black sand and the herons have a rookery. Or we could have put in at Mount Vernon, paddled down Minnehonk Lake, and threaded our way into Hopkins Stream and the lovely marshland it runs through.

I suppose the number of backyard canoe trips is finite, but I'm not at all worried. There are more than enough to fill the rest of my midsummer days, and if I ever should run out, all I have to do is just add on another half-hour's drive and enlarge the definition of my backyard a bit.

Cidering Off

I've never actually heard anybody use the phrase "cidering off," but it's high time someone did. Cider making is so much like sugaring off—and at the same time so different—that it deserves a name that reminds us of that contrary kinship. Maple syrup and cider are both tree crops; both are essences of arboreal sweetness, and, it seems to me, of the particular sweetness of the seasons that produce them.

While maple sugar is our first food crop, cider is our last, the one we can still reap after the frosts have reduced squash and tomato vines to withered wraiths of their former burgeoning selves and left brown, rattling cornstalks standing at attention in the wind like regiments of superannuated soldiers. Cider, like maple syrup, is a product of an equinox; but while syrup comes to us roughly halfway through the sun's advance toward summer, cider comes halfway through its retreat back into winter. While sugaring is a time of soft overtures and colors, of lonely vigils as the steam rises from the evaporator into a moonlit night, cidering is a time of high color and high drama, a time for melodrama even, and for the human comedy. At cidering time, those energies that were merely latent in the early spring have swelled to full force. The pastels of March are crescendos of red and gold now. The prize tomatoes, peppers, and cukes have had their day at the Grange exhibits at the county fair in September and have been duly awarded their blue ribbons. The branches of apple trees that were resplendent with pink and white flowers in May and June are heavy with fruit—round, ripe, juicy, and pungent, the stuff of which revels and celebrations and even downright orgies are made.

By late summer, the trickles of sugar that gathered in the sap buckets have, in myriad other guises, swollen to torrents. In the harvest season, it is all we can do to gather them in—to freeze and can and dry and put carrots and beets and potatoes to bed in the root cellar and squash and pumpkins in the attic. Our cup runneth over, and cidering off is the last thing we do each year to catch that overflow.

It may be possible to make cider alone with a small tub press, but in my mind that would be like going to a contra dance at which you were the only dancer. In my personal history, cidering has always been a social event from start to finish; and I can hardly imagine it otherwise. For one thing, if you want to make a lot of cider, you need to pick a lot of apples and gather a lot of sound drops. So it makes much more sense for three or four or five people to go out on a bright, breezy fall afternoon when the air is as crisp and tangy as a first bite into a Northern Spy. Ferreting out a few old Russett trees on an abandoned farmstead back in the woods is like striking a vein of gold, and though you may not want the whole world to hear about your find, you want to share your glee with some select friends. And then the work of picking bushel after bushel and of hauling your grain sacks full of apples back to the pickup truck is hardly work at all when there are many hands and lots of gabbing to lighten it.

The pressing itself, using the huge old rack-and-cloth press our neighbors up the valley have in their barn, requires a small army: two hands in the loft feed the apples into the hopper of the grinder; another hand pulls the pomace down the chute with a garden hoe; two more hands spread the cloths over the yard-square rack, load the pomace into the cloths, fold them over, then add on another rack, fill another cloth, and so on until the stack of pomace-filled "cheeses" is four or five high; then it takes three people putting all their strength into it to wind the big screw down and squeeze the cider out; and when the amber nectar gushes out of the cloths and pours out the spout in the base of the press, somebody else has to keep rotating the catching buckets, emptying them into big plastic garbage cans from which three or four more workers divvy the cider up into the gallon jugs everyone has brought to take their cider home in. After each pressing, the dry pomace is dumped into a wheelbarrow and carted out to the compost pile; and throughout the whole process everyone has to keep sampling each batch of cider, accounting for the tanginess of this batch by the predominance of Spies in it, for the zesty, astringent mellowness of that one by the balance of Jonathans and Macs and just a dash of crabapples.

There isn't a trace of alcohol in this cider yet, but everyone gets high on it anyhow. The instant gratification of each pressing and the seemingly unending flow of that fresh, cold cider that, at its best, is both sweet and dry can't but intoxicate; and the high spirits overflow into handstands, romps with the dogs and kids, chin-ups on the barn beams, and, at day's end, eating and drinking and dancing.

Cidering off with all the spontaneous revelry it generates is, I feel, a much more genuine thanksgiving celebration than the more solemn, official holiday that will follow a few weeks later. When cider pours from the press, "earth's bounty" ceases to be a cliché or an abstraction. We can roll on our tongues the energies of sun, soil, and water that the tree has brought together and concentrated in its fruit. And when we split up and take our family's share of cider home—some to pasteurize, some to make hard cider, some to make vinegar—we take with us a gift that will remind us of that bounty all through the winter months. Cider has a purity and permanence about it that our other winter stores in the root cellar do not. The mice can't get into cider and chew holes in it. It does not sprout. It does not develop soft spots and rot. It is a constant reminder, like the jars of maple syrup standing next to it, that the earth never stops bearing fruit, even when it is buried under three feet of snow. So when we sample that first cup of cider in the fall, we're tasting not just the fruits of the summer past but also an inkling of the sugar that will rise again next spring.

The End of
the Road

Aldo Leopold once said he felt sorry for the coming
generations that wouldn't have any more blank spots on
the map to explore. Now, in the days of aerial cartography,
there are no blank spots left on maps anywhere, not even
in the woolliest wilds of the wildest Canadian wilderness,
much less in our long-settled, much-overrun little New
England. But in a town at the end of a road, some of the
pleasures of living on the borders of uninhabited, if not
unexplored, territory can be yours.

On road maps, my village of Temple, Maine, sticks out
on a tiny, terminal twig of Route 43 into what is, for
anyone determined to travel only by automobile, a very
blank spot indeed. An urban mind would call this town a

blind alley, a cul-de-sac, a dead end. Go to Temple and step off the edge of the civilized world. Plunk. But what the city mouse sees as the end is, for the country mouse, just the beginning. A town like this is like a flower. The road is the stem; it takes you to the petals that reach out in all directions. For at the end of the road, any direction you choose, except the road back, takes you out where hay and potatoes and kale grow, where chestnut-sided warblers flit through the alders along the brook, where owls hoot on frost-filled November nights, where deer run and coyotes sing and just about everything else worthwhile in this life goes on. The only edge you step off is the edge of I-95 and all its tributaries, the edge of McDonald's parking lot, the edge of the power grid.

Which is not to say that all is a sylvan idyll here, that our blank spot has gone untouched by the hand of man. Along with the old county roads and stone walls and cellar holes of the past are the clearcuts and bulldozed roads and ATV tracks of the present. Even the traffic, which one would expect to be nearly nonexistent, comes as a surprise. Not all that many people live here, but any traffic on a road that goes nowhere else is automatically doubled. What goes up must come down. I'm often shocked at how many times I travel it myself.

Our town at the end of the road is hardly immune to the ills of the waning twentieth century; but, for now anyhow, we still have woods on three sides of us, not just on two or one or none. And that is not only a joy to wake up to every morning; it is also an inspiration to keep this outpost an hospitable one for loons and great blue herons and black bears and for people who need some woods big enough to get lost in at their back doors.

And then we mustn't forget one final privilege that living in a dead-end valley like this confers: If a bewildered motorist stops to ask me directions to Strong or Weld or Wilton, I can tell him, with a perfectly straight face, "You can't get there from here." Once his initial shock has abated, I add that he *can* get there. But first he'll have to go back from Here to where he came from; only then can he go on to There. An excellent piece of advice, it seems to me, for folks with nothing on their minds but getting ahead fast.

One Step at
a Time

One of life's great pleasures is connecting with people who share your appetites, aversions, perceptions, preoccupations, follies, and mad pursuits. It may be edifying and enlightening to meet someone who admires, say, the early Bergmann above all other cinematographers and can tell you why, but it is surely much more fun to meet someone who thinks, as you do, that the Marx Brothers in *A Night at the Opera* represent the zenith of film art. I feel the same kinship with people who, if told they could have only one thing to eat for the rest of their lives, would choose asparagus. Or who absolutely detest marzipan.

I don't run across people every day who share these tastes, but they do turn up. It's very seldom indeed, however, that I find anyone else who shares with me the bear-went-over-the-mountain syndrome. The name of this affliction derives from the song that tells about the bear who went over the mountain to see what he could see, and whaddya think he saw? He saw another mountain, so whaddya think he did? The bear went over the mountain to see what he could see. Etcetera.

Not too many years ago I met a man in Farmington who is as seriously affected by this psychopathology as I am, perhaps even more so. He is an otherwise exemplary professional man, citizen, husband, and father; but get him out in the bush, and he is a nut. He'll go anywhere. The more unpromising the terrain, the better he likes it. If you're standing on the edge of what looks like a square mile of alder swamp and you say, "Hey, Bill, whaddya suppose is in there?" he'll say, "I dunno. Let's go see." He doesn't limit himself to going over mountains. With him, it's more like the bear went any damn place nobody else would dream of going.

What motivates him and me and presumably the bear is the knowledge, based on much experience, that revelation comes to him or her who puts one foot in front of the other. Bushwhacking is a spiritual exercise, a form of meditation by way of the feet, not the soul; and there is no better time for it than late September. The nights are cold; the flies are gone; the air is crisp and clear, but the sun still has enough power to bake you through and let you rise up like fresh bread if you stretch out in it for half an hour on a rocky ledge. So on the last weekend of last September, Bill and I decided to go to Ironbound Pond, about thirteen miles northeast of Jackman. In the Land Use Regulation

Commission's (LURC) Maine Wildlands Lake Assessment of June 1987, Ironbound Pond drew high marks even on the list of Maine's Least Accessible Undeveloped Highest Value Lakes. By LURC's definition anyhow, Ironbound Pond is about as gemlike as any of Maine's gem lakes can get.

I'd quibble a bit about that "least accessible" epithet. Ironbound Pond may be inaccessible for a stretch limo, but if you drive a '71 Chevy Blazer you're not too fussy about—no problem. We gassed up in Jackman, headed into the woods past Jackman Mill, swung north on the road along Upper Churchill Stream, wriggled east and north past Mud Pond and Fish Pond, and dropped down into Alder Brook valley in a blinding, torrential rainstorm. But before the rain set in we had seen Boundary Bald Mountain lifting its head up above everything else in the territory and we agreed that even though we were on our way to a gem lake, these two bears were going to fit in a jaunt up that mountain before this three-day trip was over.

On the last leg of the road into Ironbound Pond you head into a tunnel of door-scratching alders and jounce along an ancient, rutted track filled with mudholes that you roar through, hoping to fly across them before you have a chance to sink in. A mile and a half of that brings you into a grassy clearing where you can camp only about a hundred yards from the pond.

Well, LURC is right about one thing. Ironbound Pond is a gem, a narrow gem about three quarters of a mile long and set down in a rocky slot between the ledges of Ironbound Mountain that rise right out of the water on the northeast shore and an almost equally steep hillside on the southwest. Beautiful it is, and dramatic and a little claustrophobic.

When Sunday morning broke sunny and clear, we set off early for a day of bushwhacking. By seven o'clock we were working our way up the west end of Ironbound Mountain, easing out onto the ledges that overlook the pond to the south, then turning east to traverse one of those lovely, high plateaus where big hardwoods have long since shaded out the undergrowth and you can walk unimpeded among the big tree trunks with the sunlight sifting down through the leaves and dappling the ferns below.

The highest ground on Ironbound Mountain is wooded, but from it we could catch glimpes of the south arm of Canada Falls Lake off to the north, empty of water now and visible only as a light green swath. And to the west was Boundary Bald, which, from this angle, seemed to rise up from the waves of the lesser hills around it like the prow of a great ship.

We started up it the next day just after noon. We had no guidebook, so we were flying by a DeLorme atlas and topo maps published in 1922 and 1956. With their help, we made our way on logging roads to the abandoned fire warden's camp and stopped there briefly for lunch. Then, with nothing else to go by, we set off on the long since overgrown warden's trail, which after a few hundred yards came out into some recent cuttings that extended, as we would find out, all the way up the lower slope of the mountain to where the krummholz began. At first we found an occasional run of old telephone wire, and spotted an insulator hung on a small tree that had escaped the loggers' saws. Then all traces of the trail disappeared in the raspberries and new growth, and we wallowed and scratched our way up the slope, making an educated guess from the map about where the trail might have gone.

Sometimes the gods are kind to bushwhackers, and they were to us. Just as we were coming out of the cuttings and onto the steepest part of the mountain where the dense, scrubby black growth would have made climbing hard for a snake, we stumbled onto the trail. From there on, it was clear sailing to the bare, open rock on the summit. And once we broke out onto that dome, all was pure brilliance and light, as if we had emerged on God's bald pate encircled for as far as the eye could see with a halo of fall color.

When the bear goes over the mountain, he can't know what it is he's going to find. But sometimes he lucks out. Sometimes he sees not just another mountain but a big swatch of Quebec to the north, and if he turns around and looks south, he sees his whole world, from Bigelow in the west to Moosehead Lake in the east, all of it spread out at his feet, Ironbound Mountain, where he has just been yesterday, and Attean Pond and a small million other hills and ponds and streams where he has been this year or last year or the year before.

I've always envied those mystics who, in moments of spiritual ecstasy, see the One in the All, the world in a grain of sand. It would be nice, on the road to Damascus or anywhere else, to have all truth revealed to you in one blinding flash. But that doesn't seem to be my way. I come to my visions one step at a time, putting one foot in front of the other. And sitting on top of Boundary Bald Mountain, sharing a handful of tiny blueberries with my friend Bill, and looking out over the glow of the Maine woods in late September, I see no reason to complain. One could do worse than be a pedestrian mystic.

A Slipping-Down Farm

There are many times in the year when I realize I am spread too thin, but right now, in mid-October, I feel like a last pat of butter that has been told to cover six more slices of bread.

I settle down after Sunday breakfast and draw up a list: Clean up garden and put it to bed. Convert five lambs on the hoof into legs, chops, roasts, and stew meat. Behead, pluck, and draw twelve chickens. Move this year's dry firewood from drying shed into wood room, thereby emptying drying shed. Cut, twitch, split next year's firewood to fill empty drying shed. Fix leak in chimney flashing. Bank north side of house. Take mowing machine off tractor. Put snowplow on tractor. Do not think about all the projects you were going to complete this summer and now have to postpone until next summer (that's a sure route to depression, a luxury you can ill afford). Sweep chimneys. Clean out stovepipes. Collect apples. Press apples. Bottle cider. Drink cider. Jack up garage and repile the rock piers so garage will not slide off them into swamp. Ask yourself for the eighty-seventh time why anybody put a garage on top of loose rocks piled in a swamp in the first place. Resolve to pour cement footings for the garage. Pray for rain so that you can curl up with a good book and do none of the above (except perhaps drink some cider that the neighbors have alread pressed). Better yet, pray for snow that will cover up all your sins of omission until next April.

I look hopefully toward the skies, but they are bright and clear. I climb up on the roof with the chimney brush and go at it. From my roof, I can see out over most of our 136 acres, taking in both their glory and their ignominy at a glance. The glory is mostly God's, and I can take no credit for it: that fall melding of birch yellow, oak brown, swamp-maple red, sugar-maple gold, and evergreen green; the meanderings of Temple Stream flowing through our land; the hills rising up steeply on either side of the valley. The ignominy lies in all those things I ought to have done here but have left undone: the fence posts, heaved by the frost, tilting every which way; the sagging page wire around the sheep pasture; the legions of chokecherry and alders surrounding the fields, ready to overrun them the instant I lower my guard. When my wife, Rita, and I bought this place thirteen years ago, the fields were run down but free of brush. Today they are still free of brush and still run down. I've held my own but not made any headway. As for the hundred-plus acres of woodland, they have tended to themselves. The dense stands of fir that should have been thinned and opened up thirteen years ago are denser than ever. A stand of red oak that was mature thirteen years ago is overmature now.

Clearly, I think, sitting astride the ridgepole, we bit off more than we could chew. The acreage and my body weight are equal: 136 acres, 136 pounds. In the past, I might have considered that a fair contest. We're both junior welterweights. But now, pushing fifty and with several of my life's fondest projects still not started, I begin to suspect that I'm outclassed.

When we bought this place, it had been slipping down for years. It was then (and still is) known as the Dana Hamlin place, for Dana lived here from 1901 until 1968. We were lucky enough to know Dana, and he showed us pictures of the place when it was in its prime and he was in his. The huge old barn was still standing. The fields were immaculate. There wasn't an alder or a stalk of goldenrod in sight. That is the image I have of this place; that's how I think it ought to be. But I forget that Dana and his wife and a hired man gave their full energies to keeping it that way. I forget that in the last ten years of Dana's time here, when he was already in his eighties and clearly had no business being here but clung to the place out of a gentle, tenacious passion for it, in those years the barn sills went down, the alders, chokecherry, and hardhack took over the stream banks and the drainage ditches and the swampy areas where you can't mow with a tractor. Somebody could always be found to knock down the grass and bale it, but only somebody like Dana in his prime would patrol the stream banks and the swales with a brush scythe.

Then Dana finally sold to a man from a neighboring town who came out on weekends and days off to gut the house so that it could be renovated from the ground up. For three years nobody lived here, and when the new owner, who worked for the state, was transferred out of this area, we bought from him. The land had gone back further still; the house was a shell with rotting sills, rotting window frames, and holes in the walls big enough to throw a cat through. Local observers advised us to knock the house down, burn the rubble, and start over again. A friend who drove up with us from Massachusetts one April weekend to see our new home threw up her hands and said, "Why are you doing this to yourselves?"

There have been many occasions since when I have wondered myself. Even in the first flush of our infatuation with this place, we knew we did not want to be full-time farmers. Both Rita I had years of literary training and work behind us. We couldn't simply abandon that, nor did we want to. We wanted some physical work and some mental work. We wanted to satisfy some (not all) of our needs for food, fuel, and shelter through our own physical efforts. For the cash we still needed, we would rely on freelance translating, writing, and editing. What we wanted, in short, was wholeness, an organic life. I almost blush to use those terms, because I and lots of other people I know have said and done some foolish things in their name. But I remain loyal to the ideas the terms represent. For all the romantic excesses the "organic life" may conjure up, it means some of the things I still think essential for a sane existence: work for the body, work for the mind, a place in the natural world and a place in the social one, some direct participation in the production of food.

We did not need 136 acres for that. Five or ten would have done nicely. But now that we've got the 136 acres, what do we do with them? In our early years here, the problem was not as pressing as it is now. The problem then was to rescue a nearly moribund old farmhouse, to clear away the brush and burdock so we could get in the front door, and to carve a garden plot out of the sod. We behaved then as if we had only five acres. We had our hands full to get the house and the grounds closest to it under some kind of control. We were thankful that a man up on the hill still had a dairy herd and wanted to hay the fields. That was all the thought and care we could give to them.

Our first ten-year plan is behind us, not all of it executed to perfection by any means, and the place is more or less livable. The house, given some reasonable care, is good for another hundred years. The sheep have not gotten onto the front porch for some time now. They stay on their side of the fence; we stay on ours. The tractor and the tools have their shed. The chickens have their coop. The garden grows. The blueberries grow. The raspberries grow. The fruit trees don't grow. We appear to be lousy orchardists.

We have imposed some order on our immediate surroundings. Within a radius of some two hundred yards out from our kitchen stove, there is clear evidence that somebody lives on this place. Beyond that, nothing is clear at all. It would seem logical that we should keep enlarging that radius until it reaches our outer boundaries. Someday, according to that logic, we should look out our kitchen windows onto lush green fields free of hardhack and swale grass. Someday we should walk through a woodlot of tall, flourishing, marketable trees with more on the way, a woodlot like the municipal forests of Rita's native Switzerland.

But all that calls for a major policy decision, a major commitment, and as I consider how I will ever meet that commitment if I take it on, I remember that Dana and his hired man worked full time on the farm and did not spend forty to fifty hours a week translating books. And if their example is not enough, I can turn to Thomas Jefferson's *Garden Book* (published in 1768), in which a correspondent named Thomas Boyne wrote to Jefferson: "It is my conclusion that the smallest farm needs two men. One may plow and sow and harvest and tend to the needs of stock. The other must needs be diligent in fence repair, battling building decay, preparing fuel and marketing the increase to advantage. If there be a boy as well, some advance may be made in clearing, cistern building or other forward tasks."

At a time when my farm is calling me to ever greater advances in forward tasks, I find that simply holding my own is about all I can do and is often more than I want to do. Time's winged chariot is doing its work; my second boyhood seems to be coming on prematurely. In my first boyhood, all I wanted to do was read, write, and run around in the woods. That's about all I want to do now, too. By the time you're fifty, you'd better know what your priorities are, even if they are regressive. Then, too, I have horrendous bouts of hay fever every June. And on top of that I'm convinced that my genetic inheritance must go back to a hunter-gatherer folk rather than to an agrarian one, which is to say I would much rather go fishing than hoe corn.

The solution many people have found to the problem of the slipping-down farm is to let their places go to hell. Fifty years ago there were forty-two working farms in the Temple Stream valley and on the hillsides around it. Dana Hamlin knew. He used to collect milk and cream from them and haul it into the railroad station in West Farmington. Today there are only two working farms nearby, and only four families (including ours) even bother to keep their fields open. Why not let the fields go back? Why not follow the example of many others who were far better, more talented, more devoted farmers than I? It is no disgrace to throw in the towel where better men have failed. And nature is smart. She will make her own good sense of my land if I do not.

That may well be, but I can't make my peace with it. Farms, it seems to me, are the closest analogue to the Creation we have. All our mythologies tell us that God or the gods made an ordered universe from incomprehensible chaos. Equipped with less than divine powers, we make smaller ordered universes out of the vast, teeming complexity of nature. Millions of animal species are more than we can handle, so we keep cows, horses, sheep, pigs. We cannot deal with the millions of plant species in nature, so we grow wheat, barley, oats, carrots, and peas. A farm is in nature and of nature but contrary to nature; it is our small gear that meshes with the greater one of creation. We have some influence, though hardly complete control, over the part of creation we have staked out as our own; but if we hold up our end of the bargain, if we stick by the land and keep our little wheel rolling, God (or the gods) will keep the big one turning, too.

To make a deliberate decision to let my own place go back, to let this one patch of land that I've taken on as my responsibility slip down even more, seems like breaking a covenant. Yet to neglect all those loud voices in my own head that say "Stop! Enough!" would be a breach of another kind. What is organic about a life that ignores its own strongest inner promptings?

If I throw all the (dwindling) spare energy I have into making this place a model New England farm, it may be the better for it, but I will be the worse. And there is no doubt, as Thomas Boyne knew, that "forward tasks" call for extra energy. You need two men and a boy, or you have to work as hard as two men and a boy yourself. The first of those solutions I cannot afford financially; the second I cannot afford physically or psychologically.

The solution is a time-honored one in northern New England: you patch and make do; steady by jerks, you move ahead; you muddle through. Jack, who used to mow the fields, is cutting down his herd and doesn't want to hay our place anymore, but Charley, the only other dairy farmer left within ten miles of us, wants to lease the fields, plow them up, reseed them, build up the humus. We see eye to eye on the care of the soil. For the next five years anyhow—and longer, if things work out—the fields will be gaining, not losing.

And what about the brush? Well, I can't say I feel all that bad about the stuff that's got a foothold along the stream and the drainage ditches. Our place is a paradise for birds, and in the spring and summer my head spins trying to spot the veeries and warblers and yellowthroats and kingbirds and catbirds and white-throated sparrows that call for my attention. And then every once in a while a great blue heron will rise majestically out of that no-good, useless alder swamp behind the house, or we'll hear a bittern's pile-driving un *go-chunk*, un *go-chunk*, un *go-chunk* rise up out of it and echo around the valley at dusk.

And if the stream banks were clear of trees and brush and down elms, where would the trout find shaded pools to lie in and what would the beaver eat and make dams of and why would a moose bother to visit a farm that had no beaver bog to wallow in?

And the woods? What about those overmature oaks and that beech on the hill across the stream and those unpruned tangles of softwood? Well, I guess I feel that where woods are concerned no management is better than poor management, and if I can't get around to cutting the trees myself the way I want to cut, and if I can't find somebody who will cut to my admittedly cranky specs, then the woods can continue to tend to themselves.

Wendell Berry has said that every farm needs a sacred grove, a place where no work is ever done, a place within ten minutes walk of the back door where we can always go and see (or at least begin to imagine) what the world was like before we ever touched a hand to it. There is no mistaking the sacred grove on our place. The hillsides dropping down into the little glen are too steep for man, beast, or machine ever to work on them, and tossed out on the glen's floor like a handful of dice are glacial erratics bigger than skidders and bulldozers, some of them bigger than houses. Porcupines den in the caves in the winter and leave quills scattered on their verandahs. A tiny rivulet runs under the snow, slips down over mossy rocks in the summer, opens into a deadwater, then into a miniature lake surrounded by marshland.

I like the idea and the reality of a sacred grove, and I may well let sacredness spread on my woodlot, for much as it pains me to see farmland go back, it pains me just as much to see every bit of land "managed" to suit the needs of humankind. Do I contradict myself? I certainly do, and at this point in my life, I've given up on achieving single-minded clarity about anything. I feel good if I can just sort out the strands of my confusion into some surveyable order.

I want to see land used and managed and productive, and I want to see land left alone. I want to see farms, and I want to see wilderness. I want my own place to be both farm and wilderness, a place where the forward tasks and the slipping down are in some kind of equilibrium, where the domestic and the wild can live hand in hand, where the lamb can lie down with the lion, where I can put down the shovel and pick up the fly rod. And what I see from the ridgepole is just that: a semicultivated semiwilderness, scruffy around the edges but hospitable to all the creatures who live on it and from it, a scene pleasing not only to bitterns and beaver but also to gods and men.

Afloat on Snow

All our most pleasurable means of travel make use of water, and when I say water, I include ice and snow—water in its solid as well as its liquid form. They also make use of what I suppose would nowadays be considered technologically rather primitive devices: canoes, sailboats, snowshoes, cross-country skis.

Travel in just about any kind of conveyance has its moments—floating above a carpet of clouds in a jetliner, for example. Or, on shipboard, watching the coast of Maine rise out of the sea. Even the lowly automobile can show you some wonderful sights as it winds down a mountain pass in Austria or, closer to home, tops Indian Hill overlooking Moosehead Lake. But for all that, I still find the *process* of petroleum-powered travel singularly dreary. One does, after all, very little but sit on one's duff and watch the landscape go by. It's a sedentary business for which passive words like "I was flown" or "I was shipped" seem more appropriate than active ones like "I flew" or "I sailed."

Travel utilizing "primitive" technologies, on the other hand, is endlessly engaging and enchanting. Part of the fascination comes, I think, from the interplay of our own minds and bodies with natural elements and natural forces. That is a rather abstract way of saying there's a thrill quite unlike any other in feeling the tug of accelerating water as it seizes your canoe at the head of a rapid, the tug of a fresh breeze as it fills your sails, the tug of gravity as you head down a hill on skis. In skiing, sailing, and paddling, there is a thrill not of conquest but of harmony, an almost musical thrill. You use skis and your own weight, sails and tiller, canoe and paddle, to play the forces of gravity, wind, or current like an instrument. The thrill is not a cheap one. It takes years of practice to play well, and if you play badly, the results can be uncomfortable, if not worse. Depending on terrain, wind, weather, and I don't know how many other variables, the demands on your own muscle power and alertness can vary hugely. Are you floating along on an easy current without a rock in sight, or are you bucking a heavy chop on a windswept lake? Are you swooping down a long, gentle slope from ridge to valley floor, or are you pushing your way up a steep trail? There are moments of ease, exhilaration, and illumination. There are moments of excruciating exertion, near-terror, and bone-weariness. There is never alienation, ennui, or isolation from land and weather.

In the winter, when snow transforms the surface of the

earth into an almost liquid one, travel in the forest becomes much closer akin to canoeing or sailing than it is to walking on bare ground in the spring, summer, and fall. Ski and snowshoe language reflects this liquefaction of the land: "flotation" is what keeps you on top of the snow, and if your snowshoes don't provide enough of it for your body weight, you'll sink. And if you go out on cross-country skis in powder snow, you'll need wide touring skis, not skinny little racers, to keep you afloat. Then, too, the motions of cross-country skiing seem almost a blend of running and swimming. The adjectives that come to mind to describe them are "liquid" and "flowing." The snowshoer, of course, does not glide. He still walks. He still has to pick 'em up and put 'em down. But even for him snow eases the way. It fills in the holes, covers up the snags, smooths out the bumps. Isaiah would have loved snow. It exalts the valleys and makes every mountain and hill low (well, not quite). It makes the crooked straight and the rough places plain.

For bears, winter may be a time of closing up and tucking in; but for human beings who avail themselves of this primitive technology, land travel is never so easy and elegant. Winter is a time of release and opening up. The landscape becomes transparent, spreading out like a map in front of you. The hillsides that are hidden from view when you walk the summer woods are right before your eyes now. You can almost reach out and caress them and feel the shape of this little valley, the backbone of that ridge. I put on my skis and go places I can't go at any other time of year. Bogs I wouldn't dream of wallowing through in the summer become oases. Places where you would slog your way through bugs and alders and knee-deep mud become highways of white silk under your feet. The water-killed spruce and fir rise more delicately and lovely than any minarets in the moonlight. The tapestry of tracks of fox and coyote and squirrel and snowshoe hare reassure you that the web of life is unbroken.

Just south of Attean Lake near Jackman is Number 5 Bog. On the map it looks to be about four miles long and four miles wide and just about one of the last places on earth you'd want to be on foot. If you beach your canoe and climb up the bank of the Moose River, which flows along the bog's edge, you'll see nothing but alders, hummocks, and mud. Not very inviting in June, but downright possible in January. Maybe this January I'll finally get up in there.

The swiftness of skis and the clarity of winter let me fit and piece my world together in a way I can't at any other time. Weld, which is so far away from my home in Temple by car, is a half-day's jaunt over Wilder Hill on the snow. If I want a couple of hours off closer to home, I can hop from Drury Pond to Pickerel Pond to Ballard Pond, skimming through the puckerbrush and beaver bogs between them where, in the summer, no way would open. In winter, my skis let me get to know my world—from my back fields to the Canadian line—with an intimacy impossible at any other time. And so I've come to feel that winter may be about the warmest season of the year after all, and my skis (along with my canoe) among the most advanced means of transportation I know.

Keeping the Loons
at Home

Black Pond is a long, narrow arm reaching north-west out of Chesuncook Lake. It is really just a widening of Caucomgomoc Stream, which runs from the lake of that name down to Chesuncook and drains an octopus-like configuration of ponds and streams that reaches north to Allagash Lake and west to the St. John watershed. When Bill Geller and I were there, it was late spring but not yet summer, and the north country was still sweet and fresh. The ice had not been out of the lake for many weeks, nor the snow off the ground, and if you looked in the right places in the woods, in shaded nooks behind rock out-croppings, you could still find packs of corn snow holding out against the heat. The leaves, still just opening out, seemed to float in the bare branches of the trees like a green mist.

We were paddling north, lazing along on a warm, windless morning, letting the power of the spring sun soak into our backs and shoulders like liniment. There would be time enough to work hard this afternoon, when we would pole up Caucomgomoc Stream and carry around the little falls about midway up. But for now, we would meander, keeping our silence, watching the osprey fish, paddling softly and slowly to ease close to the deer browsing along the shore. Since leaving camp on the bluff just north of Chesuncook we had seen six deer, three together on the east shore and three singles on the west. One, aware of us but not quite sure what to do about it, had stamped and pawed at the ground for several seconds, run a short distance, then pawed and stamped again before bounding off for good.

At the head of the pond, where Caucomgomoc Stream and the little brook from Tarbox Pond come into it, there are wide, marshy flats, and as we approached them, we saw a loon quietly swimming offshore. The flats here are not the mucky variety that suck you in over your ankles if you set foot on them. They are firm and grassy, and on this late spring morning they glowed a bright emerald green that invited us in to stroll on them. But on pulling ashore and taking a few steps, we realized, to our dismay, that we had landed practically on top of a loon's nest, though to call it a nest is a misnomer. There was no vegetation gathered or mounded up. There was not even a slight depression in the damp shore. There was just one egg, large, greenish brown, about the size of a goose egg, not the two that loons usually lay. The egg was about three feet from the water and stood out in splendid isolation on the utterly flat shoreline as if plunked down on a tabletop. Had this clutch contained only one egg from the start, or had the other been lost or destroyed? The loon we had seen on the water had not tried to lure or drive us away. Was this egg long abandoned and no longer viable? Or had our approach indeed scared the loon off the egg before we were aware of its presence? And if the egg still contained life, would the loon come back and resume incubating it again after we left? There was no way to answer any of these questions, but we moved on instantly, feeling like bulls in nature's china shop or profaners of the temple.

Whatever else that encounter did, it served as a vivid reminder of just how vulnerable the loon and its nest are in the reproductive cycle; and as if that were not quite enough, we came upon another loon nest the following spring, this time on an island in Debsconeag Deadwater in the Penobscot. There was no question about this nest. It was a large doughnut of mounded twigs and vegetation in full view on the water's edge, and perched on top of it was a loon I will not call mother loon because the males share equally in incubating the eggs. We kept our canoe a respectful distance from the nest, looking at it through binoculars; but the loon was clearly aware of us; and though it did not feel threatened enough to leave, it lay its head down on the rim of the nest and remained absolutely motionless, ready to slide off into the water if necessary.

The tiny island offered the nest some protection. It was safe from land predators, but looking at it and the brooding loon so blatantly exposed, I marveled that any pair of loons managed to stay with their eggs for the twenty-nine days needed to hatch them. And I worried about the fate of this loon family, for there is a large campsite at Debsconeag Deadwater. How many more canoes might round the end of this island in the coming weeks, and how many of them, unintentionally or otherwise, might drive the loons from their nest?

To a human mind the loon might seem stupid. If tiny songbirds are able to build far more secure nests, why does this large and powerful bird expose itself and its two precious eggs to such obvious risks? The answer is that it's primarily, if not only, the human context that makes the loon's nesting sites look ill chosen. In the millions of years of its evolution before we humans came along, those sites served it quite nicely. The loon is truly at home only in the water. It can fly, of course, but it is strictly a seaplane. Its large body, solid bones, and proportionately small wings mean that it needs a long water runway for both takeoff and landing and is suited only for straight-line flight. Like us, loons can use flight to get from place to place, but the air is not the medium in which they forage or conduct the business of life.

If loons are limited in the air, they are next to helpless on the ground. The placement of their feet at the rear of their heavy bodies makes them wonderful divers but terrible walkers. The best they can do is shuffle a few yards up on the shore, shoving their bellies along before them. Their limitations in the air and on land therefore oblige East Coast loons to leave the sea, where they winter from Newfoundland to Florida and along the Gulf Coast, and migrate to inland northern lakes to breed. Unable to land

and take off from the ground or to move all but the shortest distances on it, loons cannot nest, as other seabirds can, in rookeries well above the waves and the tides. On lakes from New England north to the Arctic they find both fish for food and the stable shorelines that support nests yet leave them easily accessible from the water. Not so dumb after all.

But if there is too much human acitivity on those lakes, if shorelines fill up with summer cottages or if too many boats disturb the loons' peace or if water levels are raised and lowered to suit human needs, the breeding cycle can be broken, no chicks are hatched, and populations decline.

It may be a cliché to speak of the loon as the symbol of the North Woods and its song as the voice of the wilderness. But clichés don't get to be clichés for nothing, and persistent symbols partake of realities as well as pointing to them. The loon doesn't just *represent* the North Woods; in some important way it *is* the North Woods. If it leaves, as it has had to leave hundreds of Adirondack and Ontario lakes where acid rain has killed off the fish, a crucial touch of wilderness goes with it. The woods are still there, but they are transformed and diminished, no longer what we know as the North Woods at all.

In recent years, the loon as a symbol of the wilderness has taken on even more significance because its survival is so clearly linked to the preservation of wild places. In its vulnerability, a nesting loon is, if you will, a sitting duck. So are the North Woods. We have to back off, give them both room, and let them be if we mean to keep our loons at home.

Summer's Boomerang

Our friend Suzy had brought the boomerang from Cambridge when she came to visit in February. It was a gift for Greg, who was twelve years old at the time and not one to postpone gratification; but after the boomerang took its second nosedive onto the icy driveway and a few splinters flew from one of its red, laminated tips, he was willing to yield to parental advice and wait for softer days and soils.

By the time summer came, Greg was thirteen. The boomerang had been circling on the outer edge of our attention for several months, first fading, then hoving into view again in the catch-all clutter of our ancient Maine farmhouse where objects appear and disappear and reappear in tune with some mysterious seasons of their own.

Then, one evening in July, when Rita had gone off to play in her recorder consortium and Greg and I were home alone with the whole spread to ourselves, the boomerang turned up in his hand. "Hey, Dad," he said, "let's throw the boomerang."

It was a perfect night for it, windstill and just starting to cool off, and the barn swallows were out cavorting, swooping, circling in quick, banking turns that invited imitation and envy.

On our first attempts, the boomerang behaved more like a mole than a swallow, heading not for the sky but for the earth, where it would often bury one of its scimitar snouts in the turf. Chastened, we finally read the instruction label. Hold the boomerang as you would a sickle, the instructions said. Throw it overhand and nearly perpendicular to the ground.

My first toss lodged the boomerang high in an old apple tree. I fetched my canoe pole and knocked it down. Greg sent the boomerang on a gorgeous outward flight that ended in a fluttering descent into tall grass. Like hunters searching for a downed bird, we worked our way out in ever widening circles from the crash site. The light was fading. It took us ten minutes and three combings of the area before Greg finally kicked the boomerang free from where it was nestled into the grass.

But there was enough daylight left. We learned how. The boomerang sailed out over the chicken coop, started its banking, side-slipping turn over the apple tree, then swung back toward us over the garden.

"Yay!" Greg yelled. "We've got it!" And he would run to retrieve the boomerang. We weren't perfect. It would not come back to our feet, like an obedient dog, so that all we had to do was lean down and pick it up. It fell fifteen yards in front of us, ten to the left of us, twenty to the right. Wherever it landed we scrambled after it to try again and again.

It was almost dark now. Our white, red-winged bird flitted out into the dusk, always returning but always taking a slightly different path, flying at a slightly different angle. July will come back again, too, but never quite this same way. Greg will never be thirteen for another July; I will never be fifty.

There is just this one summer night with the veeries belting out their cascading evensong, the sky bright blue and white, then dark purple overhead and red in the west, this hush that holds our laughter and whoops of triumph in its hands.

In Praise of Pickerel

In some angling circles, pickerel do not enjoy a position of honor. Bass, sunfish, yellow perch, white perch, bluegills, and many other fishes don't either. The mere mention of these species is sometimes enough to wrinkle the nose and curl the lip of the trout and salmon purists. The look that comes over their faces suggests that they have not only heard but also smelled something highly offensive. A friend of mine whose appetites are otherwise eclectic in the extreme once surprised me by turning down an offer of largemouth bass baked in white wine and herbs. "If I can't have trout or salmon," he said, "I don't want any fish at all."

Of all the warm-water species, though, pickerel seem to

draw the most abuse. Pickerel are long, skinny, and slimy. The pickerel has the body of an eel, the face of a platypus, the teeth of a crocodile. Its green, mottled flanks blend in with the murky weed beds where it lies in wait for its prey, silent, ominous, and lethal as a U-boat. Pickerel are sneaky, snaky, cannibalistic, just plain nasty. In the eyes of some trout fans, the pickerel is a throwback, a creature that should, by good rights, have evolved off the face of the earth eons ago and never been resurrected. In point of fact, the pickerel belongs to the same order that trout and salmon do and is, if anything, more highly advanced from an evolutionary standpoint. But no matter. It still *looks* like something from the age of dinosaurs.

The purists' enthusiasm is, of course, something I share. I, too, was taught at an early age that casting flies with a split-bamboo fly rod was the noblest form of fishing and that trout and salmon were the flycaster's noblest quarry. But the aversion for pickerel and other nontrout I did not absorb, for what I had learned even before I caught my first trout was that in the absence of fly rods and noble fish, it was better to cut a straight stick in the woods, tie a hunk of line onto it, and fish for anything that swam rather than not to fish at all. As a boy in northern New Jersey, where no trout or salmon swam in the lake across the road from my house, I learned that all fish—fish per se—were intrinsically good.

Sunnies, perch, and bluegills were the friends of my earliest childhood. Those dear, dumb fish would take just about anything I'd throw at them—bacon, a gob of bread, a hunk of red flannel. They never scorned me, so who was I to scorn them? Later, when I was eleven, twelve, thirteen, my friend John Miller and I explored all the local ponds in a tattered, leaky, crack-ribbed old canoe, out for big game: bass and pickerel. In the sticky midsummer heat, painted turtles sunbathed on rocks and logs along the shore, plopping into the water if we came too close; the hum of cicadas filled the air; and when a big pickerel hit one of our lures, it was a bit like coming face to face with an aquatic tiger in the forests of the weed beds.

So even here in Maine, where I have spent the greatest part of my adult life and where trout and salmon water is always relatively accessible, I've kept a soft spot in my heart for "inferior" fish and for the pickerel in particular, which has always seemed to me the quintessential fish of deep summer, the school-vacation fish, the lie-back-in-the-boat-and-take-it-easy fish, but also the fish that can bring some real drama into all that lollygagging, the fish that comes blasting into the sun-soaked torpor of the July afternoon like a thunderstorm, twenty-eight inches of thrashing muscle and razor-sharp teeth.

I have a soft spot in my heart for the pickerel's home ground, too—shallow, mud-bottomed ponds with no more than nine or ten feet of water at their deepest point; outlet coves in larger lakes where the silt of ages has piled up, where colonies of water lilies grow, and where the shore is ringed with the bright purple of pickerel weed; sheltered backwaters where the wind dies early in the day, the surface of the water turns glassy, and I can almost smell the scent of those submarine predators rising up to me on the still, humid air.

Like the pickerel itself, these places don't usually earn the highest ratings on our inventories of natural treasures.

The pristine mountain tarn seething with trout is more likely to be declared a gem lake, more likely to wind up in a state or national park, and rightly so. Because we are in fact at that sorry pass where we have to prioritize if we are to save anything at all, we set up our human criteria for what is most beautiful, what is most fragile, what is most precious; and we rush to protect that.

But on the ponds, rivers, and lakes of the heart and among the fish of our dreams, there are only differences, not priorities; and when I give myself up to my fish dreams and fish daydreams, I may well wind up casting a fly for trout on Allagash Lake or for landlocked salmon on the West Branch of the Penobscot. But I may just as well find myself tossing the canoe onto the car rack about five o'clock of a steamy midsummer afternoon and driving to unsung, unstoried little Parker Pond, only half an hour or so from my dooryard. And once I've bounced in to the pond on the dirt road and launched the canoe, I'll swat some mosquitoes, scratch behind my ears, put on some fly dope, and start casting a bass bug for the smallmouths that like to hang around the outlet.

There are only a couple of buildings on Parker Pond, both on the north end where the road comes in. They don't intrude on the pond, and once I'm out on the water, I forget they are there. This becomes a wild pond, and I give myself up to that near mystical state that overcomes me when I'm fishing, a state of utter calm and utter frenzy, utter absorption and utter detachment, a state of intense mental activity and focus in which the mind is blank, empty, pellucid.

And as the sun drops down red under the horizon in

the hot, sticky haze, I pick up the spinning rod and start working my way slowly along the east shore, tossing first one lure then another into every pickerely looking haunt I see. I may catch a few fish; I may catch none. Either way, it doesn't matter.

There is no moon tonight. Darkness slips in over the trees and spreads out like syrup on the silent, glassy water. I've reached the south end of the pond and the shallows where the little inlet stream comes in. It's so dark now that the tree-lined shore is a black wall, and the stumps, rocks, and weed beds are black shadows on the penumbra of the water. I've put on a Jitterbug, a fat, floating lure that burbles across the water like a baby eggbeater. Without the sound of the lure and its bubbly wake I would hardly know where water began, air ended.

It's time to quit, but I toss the lure out once more and still once more, dropping it next to a big domed rock about six feet off shore. I let it lie still for a minute. Then I twitch it, twitch it again. The water under it bulges, writhes, and churns as if a geyser had just erupted. The lure flies up into the air and plops back into the water ten feet away. Did that monster really try to take it, or did he just toss it back at me for sport? I cast again and again and again, but of course the water is dead calm. Nothing. Finally I give up and paddle slowly back across the pond, the stars glowing in the water beside me.

Tiger, tiger! burning bright, in the forests of the night.

Of Frost and
the Garden

Along about mid-August, Rita and I go through a small ritual that I will call, for lack of a better name, our Mid-August Ritual. Having noticed for a day or two that the air has been a little fresher and crisper than summer air is wont to be, and having detected just the faintest tinge of red on a few of the swamp maples we see from our kitchen window, I will say at breakfast or supper, "Well, looks like fall is here."

Rita does not have to ask me why I happen to think so. She knows I will mumble something about a nip in the air and a couple of red leaves I can see out the kitchen window. So she simply responds with her line. "Fall is *not* here," she says. "It's only the middle of August."

She's right, of course. The world will stay warm and green for several more weeks, and the day that dawns brown, sere, and leafless is still a long way off.

But I'm right, too, dammit. We sometimes have walloping frosts in late August, and there *is* a nip in the air. If you are a gardener given to optimism, you will call this time of year "late summer" and rejoice in your harvest. If you are a gardener given to gloom, you will call it "early fall" and start to worry about losing your corn patch to the coons and every last edible leaf and fruit to frost. In either case, the garden looms large in one's consciousness. It is painful enough to lose seedlings to a late spring frost; but it is even more painful, after a summer's loving care, to lose peppers and melons and tomatoes that are on the very verge of ripeness. So even in basically calm and unflappable gardeners, September breeds a little nervousness and anxiety.

I have no real right to that anxiety because I am only an auxiliary gardener. And even that is probably too honorific a title. Rita is the only real gardener in this household. She provides the brains, the green thumb, and most of the labor that goes into our family garden, calling me in only when she needs some extra hands to help turn the compost, fix the fence, or clean up in the fall. She puts in the seed order in the winter, raises seedlings in little peat pots in March and April, puts them out on the porch by day, takes them in at night. She forks up the soil, makes raised beds, plants, weeds, waters, mulches. On every day that spring and summer weather allow, she spends at least a couple of hours in the garden.

My major involvement with the garden is eating what comes out of it, which I do with great appreciation, from the first stalk of asparagus in the spring to the last brussel sprout in the fall. I'm so addicted to garden-fresh lettuce and peas and beans and broccoli that if Rita decided next spring that she couldn't bear to garden another year, I would probably leap in and do my poor best, reluctant gardener that I am, rather than forgo the garden's gifts.

When September comes, then, with its erratic frosts, I feel suddenly protective of the garden: I want to keep eating fresh lettuce as late into the fall as is humanly possible, and I can't remain indifferent to the fate of living things that my mate has nurtured all summer long.

So I join her in a nightly weather consultation. Is it one of those clear, windstill nights when the cold air will roll down the hills into Temple Valley, knocking our garden for a loop while it leaves the gardens of our hillside-dwelling friends untouched? We consider the rules that have been handed down to us and try to interpret them in the light of each evening's sky. Early in our years in Temple we were told that if the temperature was 45 degrees by ten o'clock, then frost was sure. But what if there is heavy cloud cover and it looks as if rain is coming in? We learned only recently that the full moon does not in fact portend an especially cold night, but the superstitions of a lifetime are hard to shake, and we remain terrified of full moons.

When in doubt, cover up. We have a lot of old lightweight blankets, an old army poncho, some worn-out mattress pads, even some of that white, filmy Reemay stuff designed for this very purpose. Plants may not run around, but trying to dress them for the cold is a bit like trying to get a kindergarten class into snowsuits. When we think we're all done, somebody is always missing a mitten or a boot or a scarf. The Reemay doesn't reach quite far enough to cover the last two tomato plants. No matter what ingenious geometrical configuration we lay our old blankets in, a few tentacles from that squash hill are still crawling out from under them. And so we clothe those last naked strays in enough discarded T-shirts and pajama tops to make the garden look like a gathering place for headless ghosts.

But then, of course, we miscalculate sometimes. We go to bed utterly confident that there will be no frost, yet wake to a world decked in white. As long as the sun has not yet come up over the hill, there is still time to send the fire brigade to the rescue. I jump into my clothes, stumble out the door, turn on the outside faucet, and run to the business end of the hose down by the garden, ready to cleanse deadly rime from every last tender leaf. No water. I forgot to drain the hose last night, and the water left in it has frozen into icy plugs.

I coil the hose, race into the house with it, dunk it in hot water in the bathtub, knead it, bend it, pulverize the ice, race back outside again, hook up, turn the water on, pray. The hose splutters, heaves, vomits little corks of ice onto the lawn. Once it's running free, I screw the nozzle on without taking time to turn off the water. I'm drenched. Between the cold water and the frost, my hands are numb, but the hose is working, spewing its life-giving rain onto slender tomato vines and squash leaves the size of elephant's ears. By the time I feel the first hint of the sun's warmth on my back, every last plant is rinsed clean and green. There will be a little mortality, a few wilted and withering leaves, but most of the troops have pulled through. Our salad days are not over yet, not today, maybe not even this week or next.

OF FROST AND THE GARDEN

And while all this jousting and sparring with Jack Frost is going on, we're gradually gathering the fruits of Rita's work into safety: cartons of squash and of ripe and partially ripe tomatoes that we spread out on sheets of plastic in various upstairs corners, baskets of beets and potatoes and carrots to store in the cellar, onions to lay out and dry on the porch, red cabbages to wrap in newspaper. Not to mention the peas and green beans and broccoli and cauliflower and chard and raspberries and blueberries already in the freezer.

Finally, that black, killing frost comes; and when it comes—let's admit it—we heave a sigh of relief. Our tug-of-war over the garden is finished for another year, and the other team has won, as it always does. Though to speak of winning and losing where the garden is concerned is to speak in terms that do not apply. The garden has just gone into hibernation, and we will be living off its stored fat all winter, still eating the yield from this year when it's time to plant again next year. With tomatoes in our bedroom, potatoes in our cellar, and parsnips still out there in the ground where we will dig them up through the snow in April, the demise of the garden is far from a tragic event. In Maine, the official growing season may be short, but there is no end to the gardening season, as any gardener who is munching on her own carrots as she peruses a seed catalog in January can tell you. So when we speak of a black, killing frost, we are just indulging our usual human love of hyperbole. There's nothing truly black or truly killing about it. It just marks the time when both we and the garden can put up our feet and take a little breather.

North Woods
Soul Food

I don't do a lot of cooking. Rita is so good at it and so far ahead of me that I have despaired of ever catching up. But I have a few specialities, and whenever there is a call for them I roll them out. I make a superb biscuit; and immodest as it may seem, I have to say that my doughnuts are the best I've ever eaten. Breakfast guests at our house may think they've had better doughnuts elsewhere, but if that's what they do think, they've been considerate enough to keep that opinion to themselves.

My doughnut recipe comes from Amy Tufts. So does my biscuit recipe, come to think of it. I'm sorry to say I never knew Amy Tufts, but that doesn't lessen my respect for her. Her recipes were passed on to me by my old friend

Don Yeaton. Don, who was some thirty-five years my senior, had spent most of his life in the woods in lumber camps and sporting camps; and though he wasn't much of a cook either, he could recognize a good doughnut or biscuit when he ate one.

All Don ever told me about Amy was that she was a woods cook and an awful nice woman. Realizing that he might have to produce biscuits and doughnuts on his own some day, he had asked her for her recipes and recorded them on a piece of paper he kept in the drawer next to his bed in the guides' camp at Big Jim Pond. That paper was yellowed around the edges by the time I saw it, and the paper I copied my copy of those recipes onto is yellowed around the edges now, too.

I've never taken the trouble to compare Amy's recipes with Betty Crocker's or Fanny Farmer's. It would be terribly simple to do, but I don't want to take the chance of finding out that Amy's doughnut recipe is really just the basic, universal doughnut recipe you'll find in any old cookbook. It is important for me to know—or believe— that the doughnuts I fry up in my kitchen in Temple have a pinch more cinnamon or a tad less nutmeg than just any old doughnut, and that they are shoots off a distinguished family tree that goes back via Don Yeaton and Amy Tufts to a farm kitchen in Kingfield, where all the Tuftses I ever heard of come from, and then back beyond that far into the mists of unrecorded doughnut time. I experiment a little with the recipe sometimes—two whole eggs instead of four egg yolks, yoghurt instead of buttermilk, half wholewheat flour instead of all white—but the basic structure is the same. It's like building a canoe on a fine old form:

Each builder keeps the classic lines but adds a personal touch here and there.

It's important for me to know too that the doughnuts I'm still making today are essentially the same doughnuts that filled the lodge kitchen at my father's hunting and fishing camp on Big Jim Pond with fresh-fried fragrance, the same doughnuts that fortified generations of guests and guides and kitchen girls and cabin girls, the same doughnuts that fueled Don Yeaton and me as we cut camp wood in the summer, patched boats, built log camps, and cleared trails.

Doughnuts are a staple of the north country. You snatch one off the breakfast table and hang it over your thumb as you head out for work in the morning. If your day gives you ten minutes off anywhere near the kitchen, you pour yourself a cup of coffee and reach into the doughnut jar. If you'll be away all day, you stick a couple into your lunch bag. They are a year-round food, but they are especially warming for body and soul in cold weather. I don't know exactly what the caloric count of Amy Tufts' doughnuts is, but I suspect it adds up to a pretty sizable jolt, and I know how welcome it is on a windy November day when half-rain, half-snow is slicing down out of a gray sky and you're wrestling Rangeley boats onto their winter racks, draining the water pipes to the camps, and digging hunters' stuck Oldsmobiles out of mudholes on woods roads.

When bears den up for the winter they may have three or four inches of fat on their backs and rumps. When Don Yeaton and I waved good-bye to the last hunter and settled into our winter lair at Jim Pond, we had our fat stored in the form of lard, flour, and sugar. There's a story, perhaps apocryphal, that documents how important to survival doughnuts are in the North, or at least how important somebody thinks they are. In a particularly tough winter in the Yukon, the hunters and trappers were unable to bag any big game and were reduced to living entirely on hares, which are notoriously lean little creatures, all protein but no fat. By spring, everybody in the territory was skin and bone except for one old trapper who had supplemented his diet of hare with a steady supply of greasy doughnuts.

Doughnuts are rarely so essential to the body in Maine, but they are surely one of our great soul foods. Don and I fried up three dozen at a time. We had them at breakfast and with our last "lunch" about ten at night. The last half dozen of each batch were hard as rocks by the time we got to them, but they could be dunked into edibility, and the fact that they were way past their prime didn't matter much. Even old and stale and dense, they were still redolent of a freshness and warm crispness they had when lifted right out of the fat.

Doughnuts are a small luxury in a world where small luxuries are appreciated. They are the last few minutes of talk and ease you have over your final cup of coffee in the morning. They're a touch of sweetness on a sour day, a bit of fat when things are lean. They mean moments of gabbing and kidding around with your friends or family or, if you happen to be on the road, with the guy sitting at the counter next to you. And that's why I never or hardly ever pass up a chance to sample homemade doughnuts anywhere, like those huge ones in the glass jars in Thompson's Restaurant in Bingham or the ones in Evelyn's Pastry Shoppe and Bakery in Guilford, where the guys from the mill across the road drop in for their morning and afternoon coffee. And even if the product isn't quite up to Amy Tufts' recipe fried in my own kitchen, I'm never disappointed because the best things about a doughnut are, like the hole in it, invisible things that the doughnut makes visible.

Living a Dog's Age

My father was a gentle misanthrope who was not overly impressed with the behavior of his own species, and whenever he was confronted with new evidence of human greed, skulduggery, or just plain nastiness he was fond of saying, "The more I see of people, the better I like dogs." Impressed at an early age with the superiority of canine character over human, I've always seen to it that I had a dog whenever circumstances allowed. They allowed again, after many years of doglessness, when Rita and I settled on our old farm in Temple, Maine.

Our idiom tells us that a dog's age is a long time. It doesn't seem so to me. Dogs' lifespans vary just as any creature's can, but for some reason I have always thought of a dog's age as thirteen years. Of the two dogs who have been our son, Greg's, companions from his infancy and who have shared most of our life together as a family, one is dead now, and the other is enjoying a comfortable and idle old age. Her eyes are clouded with cataracts; she is so deaf you have to go up and tap her on the shoulder to get her attention; she has a patch of bare skin on her rump with a hideous but benign growth on it; she spends most of her time sleeping in her favorite spots around the house: next to my desk, under the kitchen table, under the piano (she bangs her head against it occasionally, setting the strings vibrating in a soft, doggy chord). But if you go up to her and shout "Walk!" into her ear, she will perk up. She'll get to her feet slowly, but once out the door, she'll head for the woods with a real spring in her step. There is, as the phrase has it, life in the old girl yet.

It was not until our dogs were quite old that I realized I had never shared a dog's age before. The dogs I had had in my boyhood all met premature and violent deaths; none of them lasted past four years. I had no experience of old dogs beyond seeing an occasional graybeard emerge from under a porch to woof dutifully at a stranger before returning to his nap. And having had no experience of them, I also had no appreciation of them. "Why," I would ask myself, "don't these people put this poor, doddering, cloudy-eyed, stiff-legged creature out of its misery?" But now I've seen our own dogs pass from youth to age in what seems a matter of minutes, and I know their aging years have been far from miserable ones.

On a gray January afternoon of our first winter here, we looked out the kitchen window at dusk to see a lean, wild creature leaping up at the onion bag full of suet we had hung out on a tree limb for the birds. The snow was three or four feet deep, and when the dog jumped the snow gave way under its feet. Its prospects for a meal were not good. The fat was just too far off the ground, but the dog persisted.

"That's one hungry dog," I said.

"Poor baby," Rita said, and immediately started concocting a bowlful of leftovers.

"If you feed it," I said, "we'll have a dog."

She did, and we did, and we still do. The dog was a young female of uncertain ancestry, but her coloration, head, and overall shape suggested a large dose of German Shepherd. Broad paws, a little beard she sported on her chin, and the texture of her coat, which had a soft curl to it, all hinted of Airedale somewhere on the family tree. Investigation quickly revealed that the people who were her nominal owners were only too glad to be rid of her. We tried out various names on our bearded lady, finally settling on Furry Face (or Miss Furry or Furry Dog or just plain Furry). She answered happily to any of those names or any other name, if she felt like it. If she didn't, she wouldn't.

From her ex-owners we learned that Miss Furry was about six months old, still a young dog but way past the imprinting stage. The one indelible lesson she seemed to have learned by then was that human beings might feed her and make a fuss over her but that they might also (as her previous owners had) beat the socks off her and lock her up in the back shed. With the feeding kind of humans, she was all charm and affection. But at the first hint of a

87

harsh tone in anyone's voice she melted out of sight with the skill and speed of a coyote.

There was a magic circle within which she was the most domesticated of dogs, but beyond which she was completely wild, independent, intractable. The circle had a radius of about thirty feet. If she had her heart set on chasing snowshoe hares, she would head for the edge of the circle at an inconspicuous, head-down, tail-down trot, pretending that she was invisible. If I called her in time, she would come back, tail awag, to roll over on her back at my feet. If I hesitated and she made it over the line, I could cajole, wheedle, roar authoritatively. Nothing would work. She loped on her way, tail and head high now, ears turned back to enjoy the symphony of curses following her into the bush. I swear she giggled as she ran.

In her youth she was a ferocious hunter but not the kind that would be of much use to human hunters. Like any wild creature, she hunted for reasons purely her own. This place, like most neglected old farms, was supporting a large woodchuck population when we arrived here. The summer after the winter Miss Furry joined us there were no more woodchucks. The brush and overgrown stone walls resounded with wild barking. Those big Airedale paws went to work like steam-driven entrenching tools. The dirt flew. When she caught a chuck, I could hardly believe that this growling, snarling beast, shaking and tearing its prey to pieces, was the same dog that had won the reputation of the greatest canine schmooze and baby on the whole Temple intervale.

Nothing stopped her. She had so many run-ins with

porcupines that I lost count. We wrapped her in a blanket, sat on her, plucked quills from nose, lips, tongue, and gums. She yowled so piteously that it seemed impossible she would ever forget which creature had been responsible for this agony. But she did, time and again. Miss Furry and I once put up a bear from its bed in shoulder-high grass. She was after it like a streak, no questions asked; and I'm convinced that she would have attacked it if she had ever brought it to bay, darting at it, leaping back, barking, her tail whirling propellor-like in her frenzy of delight. When Miss Furry was in her prime, I was treated to perhaps the greatest displays of youthful energy, exuberance, adventurousness, and high spirits that I've ever seen in my life. She was, in short, wonderful company, a lively, affectionate, though sometimes rather nutty and recalcitrant friend.

The affection she lavished on us she lavished just as effusively on anyone else who fed her or had a kind word for her, and within a few weeks of moving in with us, she had charmed not only us but all our neighbors as well. There were two families she was particularly drawn to. One was our friends Mitch and Sandy, with whom we do a lot of neighboring and who were instantaneously smitten with Miss Furry. We were at their place or they were at ours so often that it was only natural for Furry to think of their place as hers, too. Her other regular stop was with the Griffins, an elderly couple whom she won over so completely that they fed her steak bones, mashed potatoes and gravy, and even let her sleep on their bed. We refused to supply that kind of decadent luxury, and Miss Furry was soon spending three and four days at a time at the Griffins. "She's an awful knowin' dawg," Hilma Griffin said of her.

What she knew best, I was beginning to suspect, was how to look out for Number One. "Faithless hussy," I would grumble to myself, "whoring after mashed potatoes and gravy. You'd still be in the gutter if it wasn't for us." But whenever Miss Furry returned after a few days at the Griffins' fleshpots and told me she still loved me and asked if I still loved her and if everything was still like old times between us, I said yes, I did, and yes, everything was. I was putty in her paws.

Granted, I was a complete sucker for her, but I was also beginning to realize she had created a bond between us and the Griffins that would never have been so strong without her. Before Miss Furry became their dog as well as our dog, we had been good neighbors (as in "Good fences make good neighbors"). But it was our shared affection for her that made us all see how much more we shared as well.

Just how intent Miss Furry was on creating and maintaining an extended family became clearer still after we got Peppy, our second dog, a few years later. He came to us from overworked friends who had a dairy farm and had reluctantly inherited him from a neighbor who had moved away. For several weeks, Peppy had watched Rita come to the barn to buy milk. He knew a soft touch when he saw one, and on a particularly vile February afternoon when the wind was screaming out of the northwest, he crept out from behind a snowbank and stood cringing with his rump to the wind just as Rita emerged from the milk room. He had a genius for looking pathetic, and when he turned his soulful little face to Rita that afternoon, she opened the car door for him. Without even waiting to be asked, he got in.

Peppy's lineage was as indeterminate as Furry's and even more difficult to guess at. He was about the size of a Border Collie but had a fuller face. His long, silky, black, white, and gray coat made him look heavier than he was. The minute you touched him, you realized how slight and fine-boned he was. I suspect he had some Poodle blood in him, too, evident not in any external features but in the brightness of his eyes and expression, his playfulness, his eagerness to learn and to please.

He was as different from Miss Furry as he could be. He was no hunter, for example (though he was murder on the village garbage cans). And where Furry turned on the charm for everyone and anyone, Peppy was a one-man dog, or rather a one-woman dog. Rita had plucked him away from a cold barn and brought him to a home where he was well fed and loved. He repaid that kindness with utter, unswerving devotion.

We had only the vaguest notions of Peppy's age when he came to us. Maybe he was four or five, but he still had a puppyish streak in him, and he kept it right up until his last weeks. He loved to chase dry leaves in the fall when the wind blew them across the lawn. He would go bounding after one, pounce on it with his forepaws, then set off in pursuit of another. The leaping and pouncing were reminiscent of the movements wolves and coyotes make when they hunt rodents, and I suppose you could argue that the scurrying leaves triggered a hunting response in Peppy. I would argue instead that he knew very well what

91

a poor meal dry leaves make, and that he thought it was just plain fun to chase them.

Miss Furry and Peppy took to each other instantly, but after sharing our place with Peppy for several months, Miss Furry's visits around the neighborhood grew longer and more frequent. Finally, one day, she packed her bag, picked up her toothbrush, and left for good to move in with Mitch and Sandy. She no doubt realized that permanent residence at the Griffins' would mean living higher off the hog than even her hedonistic blood could stand, so she chose a day-to-day life of sober habits and came back down the hill to the Griffins' only when she felt the need to be shamelessly pampered (a need she continued to feel quite often).

We had been careful not to show any favoritism when Peppy arrived, but that was not good enough for Miss Furry. She clearly felt that any dog who had the vast stores of love for humankind that she did deserved the exclusive attention of any family she favored with that love. She bore no ill will toward Peppy for moving in on her territory, nor did she ever reproach us for taking this interloper into our hearts. She just moved on while still maintaining the friendliest of relations. She visited frequently, played with Peppy, joined us on hikes, and came to spend weekends or whole weeks with us if her new family was away. It was the most amicable divorce I have ever witnessed.

Greg turned ten, then eleven, then twelve. Peppy's raids on the village garbage cans became less frequent. Furry, after setting off in furious pursuit of a squirrel, would bark up its tree a few times, then turn away as if saying, "Oh, well, it's just a squirrel." The Temple hills no longer rang for hours at a time with the yelps and whoops of her nocturnal hunts. But the thing that struck us most about the dogs' aging, the thing that made us realize they actually were aging, was their new behavior on walks. Whenever we went out for a brief ramble on foot or on skis, the dogs would not disappear in wild forays through the woods. They would sniff, explore, squat, lift a leg, run a bit ahead, fall a bit behind, but they were never out of touch. If they were not in sight, we could at least always hear their tags jingling in the brush, and a call would bring them instantly loping into view. The magic circle now was not one they wanted to escape but one they wanted to remain within. The call of the wild was fading; the call of hearth, companionship, and creature comfort was growing stronger.

This past winter we put Peppy down. He was diabetic; he had kidney and prostate trouble; his attempts to pass stool were usually futile and always painful. Our vet came to the house, and Peppy went to sleep, awash in his family's tears.

Miss Furry, on her regular visits from her other home, soon took in that Peppy was no longer around. She began to stay with us for a night or two, then for three or four. Soon she was a permanent guest, and we and our friends up the hill realized that she had decided to come back to the home of her youth. It never would have occurred to them to try to hang on to her or to us not to take her back.

As these changes and passages overtook Rita and me, evoking in us a tangle of amusement and regret, delight and sorrow, we came to realize that we too were on the brink of becoming old dogs ourselves. The years we've shared with Peppy and Furry have taken us from our late thirties to our early fifties. The dogs' transition from reckless, ebullient, extravagant expenditures of seemingly endless energy to a husbanding of strength, a savoring of small pleasures, has coincided with a similar, if much slower, process in our own lives. Where I used to hike twenty-five miles in a day, I find that twelve or fifteen will do very nicely now. And if the weather looks too inhospitable, the appeal of a warm bed may win out over the lure of the trail for me, too, just as it does for my one remaining dog.

I've read recently that the old scheme of reckoning seven years of human life for each one year of a dog's life is passé now and that by the new and more scientifically correct scale, Miss Furry's thirteen years do not add up to ninety-one but to a mere girlish eighty. But whatever the scale, the whole arc of her life is present to me in one sweet, single image, like the flight of a baseball leaving the bat, soaring up into the sky to hang there briefly, then plummeting swiftly into the stands. When I watch her amble around the house now, then wriggle gleefully on her back in the grass, I can also see her racing through the woods in her youth and tearing woodchucks limb from limb. A *memento mori*? I suppose so, but a *memento vivere* as well. Life, she tells me, is good. It is just as good now, at thirteen, as it was then, at two or three.

Miss Furry will live until she dies. Go thou and do likewise, she says. I may be a bit dense if I need a dog to remind me to do that. But I do, and I hope I won't forget it in however many dog's ages are left me.

The Perfect Winter

I seem to be undergoing an atypical evolution: As I get older, I like winter more and more. At a time in life when most other folks start yearning for winters in Florida, I perk up when the first real snowfall comes and feel real regret when the dry powder of deep winter shows the first signs of turning to clabbery spring mush.

Why this is I don't know. Perhaps it has something to do with entering the winter of one's own lifetime and so feeling an affinity with the outside world. Perhaps it's an understanding that winter is not a time of "death" at all, but a time when vitality becomes all the more vivid against the clean backdrop of snow and cold. A kind of focus and clarity is possible that is not possible in the

95

fecundity of spring and summer or the blaze of fall. The sun is never warmer or brighter than on a cloudless, wind-still day in February with the temperature around zero.

A key element in the perfect winter, of course, is perfect winter weather; and because I am writing now at the tail end of a thoroughly wretched winter, I realize by comparison just how perfect the previous winter was and how rare a perfect winter is. The frequent heavy snows of January a year ago (one per weekend) built up a high, snug collar of insulation around the foundation of the house and formed the huge snowdrift outside our kitchen windows that acts something like a ski jump for the north wind and sends it shooting over the rooftop instead of slamming into the house. A lot of snow makes for a warm winter in the wind tunnel of the Temple intervale.

The temperature stayed cold enough to keep the snow powdery, yet it was warm enough that you could live outdoors with utmost comfort: ten below at night, occasionally twenty below, and no more than twenty above in the day. No thaws, no rain to turn it all to slop and then to ice and wretched crust.

And then came a halcyon February filled with bright blue skies. Halcyon days, I know, are supposed to come around the winter solstice; and in Greece, where the word "halcyon" comes from, perhaps they do. But last year in Maine they came in February, making it all but impossible to stay indoors and work. On many days they did make it impossible. In terms of strength or weakness of character, I suppose I have to say I yielded to temptation. Looking at it another way, which is the way I choose to look at it, I was wise enough to accept the gifts that a gracious universe sent my way.

96

I skied the backcountry with my friends; I skied alone; I skied with Rita. I skied all day, half a day, sometimes just half an hour. I followed the waterways, topped the hills, swooped down the slopes, sat in the sun on the shores of tiny ponds and, between mouthfuls of cheese and bread and peanut butter, said, "Thank you—whoever or whatever you are—for this day. Thank you for the good company of my sidekick Roger (or Bill or George or . . .). Thank you for this solitude. Thank you for the snow-covered dome of that beaver lodge, the swoop of the owl through the trees."

And then, after weeks of snowlessness, March 1, which was a Sunday, brought snow, a soft, steady, all-day snow; and Greg's friends came over in the morning, and they talked and listened to tapes upstairs in his room. And in the afternoon, Rita and I went out on skis up Temple Stream Valley. The world was wrapped in a snowfall silence that is not a total silence but one full of whisperings and intimations. If you stand near beech trees, which cling to their dry leaves tenaciously and often have some all winter long, and if the consistency of the falling snow is firm enough, then you will hear just what it was we heard in the woods that afternoon.

I watched Rita's slim, jaunty little shape tooling down the hills, her wool hat sticking up in the air, her mittens like paws on her poles. We glided along and stopped and grinned at each other like perfect dopes and agreed that we had been terribly clever to marry each other and choose to live precisely the kind of life we were living in the very place we were.

And when we got home we told the kids that if there was a snow day the next day, we would go downhill skiing at Saddleback together. When we made that offer, it was an expression more of fond hopes than of realistic expectations. It had been snowing all day, and we didn't believe it would continue through the night. But when we woke at a few minutes before six, Rita said, "Turn on the radio," and I did, and the guy said "It's six A.M. on this snowy, blowy Monday morning, and here's the list of cancellations. Topping the list is School District 9. No school in District 9 today. And no school either in District 58 . . ."

So we went up to Saddleback where the parking lot had some cars in it but was not full and where the lodge had some people in it but was not packed and where the slopes were not Grand Central Station but still rang with the delighted whoops of folks skiing in some of the sweetest powder Maine has ever seen.

It was downhill skiing at its natural and human best. There was no mob, so people were unhurried, friendly, talking easily and openly with whoever happened to share their chair on the lift. I couldn't help thinking that if Saddleback's overly ambitious owner had been on the slopes that day, enjoying a ski area that is still operating on a human scale and in proportion to the carrying capacity of the mountain, he might give up his lunatic dreams of making Saddleback the Aspen of the East. It's bad enough that we have an Aspen in the West.

Greg and his buddy Michael rode up the chairlift singing Talking Heads songs ("I was born in a house with the television [pause] ON . . ."). And I even made a quantum leap forward in my own skiing. I started downhill skiing late in life and with all the inhibitions of the middle-aged who do not want to break bones and twist ankles. But on that day, I learned to give myself up to gravity—to submit, in the great wisdom of Conrad's phrase, to the destructive element. And so I found safety and sustenance and, if the word is not too presumptuous, enlightenment—illumination certainly, and a lightening in another sense, the sense of a burden lifted from my shoulders. I've felt it elsewhere—in a canoe, on mountaintops, deep in the bush, in front of my typewriter. I had doubted I'd ever feel it on downhill skis, but I did. And it was one more pearl on the string of the perfect winter that lasted precisely one month longer and was then washed away overnight in the great April Fool's Day flood of that year. I didn't know whether to read that as an omen or not.

Coming to Rest
on Katahdin

April isn't the cruelest month at all. Not only is it beautiful to look it; it's also when fishing season opens in Maine and (usually) the only month in the year when you can go cross-country skiing one day and whitewater paddling the next. It's also the month when I start thinking seriously about Baxter State Park again. I rarely get up to the park in the winter, and even in the rest of the year I don't go there as often as I would like. From my home in Temple, it's a good three hours to the south gate at Togue Pond, a good four to Matagamon Gate at the northern end, which is the end I'm most drawn to these days. Call it a 350-mile round trip, not a jaunt you're likely to take for a day hike, and one you think twice about even for a long weekend. But every time I do go, I wish it was closer by. I know familiarity would not breed contempt.

A phrase that park director Buzz Caverly uses a lot is "the magnets of Katahdin," referring to the power the mountain holds over its devotees, drawing them back to it again and again. I know what he's talking about, but for me the magnets are not just of Katahdin but of *Katahdin-auguoh*, which Thoreau says is what the Indians called the whole territory around Katahdin. Governor Baxter must have felt this, too. He clearly perceived everything from Katahdin north to Webster Stream and Grand Lake Matagamon as one place, a world of mountains, ponds, brooks, and streams that he thought it worth a lifetime of effort and anxiety to assemble and protect as an unbroken whole.

To say that this gathering of mountains, with Katahdin as its crown, is like no other place in Maine is, perhaps, to waste words on the blatantly obvious. Any fool can see that. No matter how you happen on it—whether you come to it from the south on the road from Millinocket or see it rise up into the sky as you paddle down the West Branch into the head of Chesuncook or see it from the east on the height of land below Patten, where all the mountains in the park seem to gather like waves in a green sea and crest in the tidal wave of Katahdin itself—no matter how you look at it or where you look at it, Katahdinauguoh fills the eye and the soul.

There just may not be any white man's noun that can do justice to Katahdin and all its brothers and sisters towering over the low, rolling potato country to the east and north, over the lake country to the north and west. Why this lifting and heaving of the earth right here? The mountains of the park sit in a great circle like a council of giants. Start with Trout Brook Mountain in the northeast corner and head south over Billfish and Bald and Barrel Ridge to the hydra-headed Traveler massif. Let your eye wander on down to Katahdin itself, then swing north again over the Brothers and Black Cat and South Branch Mountain and back to where you started from. And in the middle of that council circle are the crystals of Pogy Pond, Weed Pond, and Russell Pond bedded in the mossy green of the Wassataquoik Valley. You don't have to be a spooky type to see, or at least imagine, this as a gathering place for the spirits of the earth. Katahdinauguoh lifts its many heads above all the lesser hills around it and announces itself to all the world as a sacred place.

On my last trip to Baxter I was with my friend Doug Dunlap, who once lived in Island Falls, about twenty-five miles due east of the park. His farm was one ridge over from the lookout in Patten, and for ten years he saw Katahdin on every day it could be seen. "It was always the same but never the same," he says. "With every slight shift in the weather or the light it would look just a little different. God, what a presence it was, white in the winter, sticking its head up above the clouds in the spring, or just a pale blue silhouette in the haze of summer. You don't forget sights like that."

The day that Doug was reminiscing about his years in the magnetic field of Katahdin was a steamy, sticky day in July, and we were climbing South Branch Mountain. The trailhead is at South Branch Pond, where one of the largest campgrounds in the park is located, and in the few minutes it had taken us to park the car, fill our water bottles, and say hello to Ranger Keith Smith, we had run a small gauntlet of Civilization and Its Discontents.

Item: Wife, sitting next to husband on campground dock, says, "Gee, isn't that a pretty point across the pond? Maybe we could paddle over there this afternoon."

Husband to wife: "Jesus Christ, what a stupid idea."

Item: Small boy about six, singing to himself, whirling his life jacket around on his wrist, and obviously enjoying himself immensely gets clobbered on the back of the head by his Old Man, who says, "Shuddup, dammit. You're getting on my nerves."

Item: Two boys about eleven years old dabbling in the outlet stream at the trail crossing say to us, "Are you gonna climb that mountain? What a boring mountain. You'll be sorry you ever climbed that boring mountain."

After that interlude among all those folks having such a good time on their vacations in the North Woods, we settled happily for the boredom and tedium of the trail. South Branch Mountain does not give away all its gifts at once. You don't break out onto any extended, bare ridges that let you walk for half an hour with a 360-degree view. Instead, there is a small opening to the north; then, a mile farther on, another short stretch of ledge that gives you your first view to the east onto Little and Big Peaked Mountains and the Travelers. These are obviously not the great, high mountains of the West, but the cliffs and columns of red rock you see across the valley have something of Arizona and New Mexico about them. And tucked down in the sharp cleft of the valley is the bright blue hourglass of Upper and Lower South Branch Ponds,

103

linked by the slim waist of the thoroughfare between them. If this be boredom, may I die of it.

As we make our way over the two main peaks and onto the bare southern end of the mountain, the view opens up to the Turners and, to the west, across Black Brook Mountain and down into Hathorn Brook Valley. It is a great comfort to me to know that this is healed and healing land I am on. These valleys I'm looking down into have been logged before, but they are not being logged now and have not been for many years. It is a great comfort to know that if I struck off on what would be a killing bushwhack to the north or south, the east or west, I would find nothing for several miles but woods and water and rock. And thinking of that, thinking how much at home that knowledge makes me feel, I recall a story Doug told me the night before at our camp on Long Pond.

Not long after he moved to Island Falls, he said, an elderly man had become "lost" in the park and never been found. The man had come into the park alone, set off on a day's hike alone, and simply disappeared. There was some speculation that he had meant to disappear, that he had deliberately slipped off into some wild corner of the park to find the grave he wanted.

Looking out over these miles of steep, densely wooded country that is at once as hospitable as it is inhospitable, as much a home and resting place as it is a forbidding northern jungle, I could easily follow that man's footsteps and feelings if he did in fact walk to a grave of his own choosing here. Where else but on park land can a man be sure his blood and bones will go back to the earth? Where else can he be sure he won't be locked up to rot in boxes of steel and cement? Where else can he be guaranteed that a shopping mall or a ski lift will not rise on his ashes or a skidder roll over his face?

Governor Baxter understood those feelings, too, just as he understood that the three hundred and some square miles of the park he created were a place where forces from the core of the earth and the heights of the sky had been gathered and concentrated as with a great magnifying glass. To be alive here is a great privilege, and to lie down and die here is a great privilege, too. Knowing that, Percival Baxter asked that his ashes be scattered on Katahdin; and he would surely have known what that lost man was seeking and what he no doubt found when he made his last camp bed somewhere among the spruce and granite and sheep laurel and slept his last sleep under the brightening stars of the evening sky.

The Top of
the River

When I'm paddling a canoe, which is something I do as often as I possibly can, I try my best to stay on top of the river. In the moderate water temperatures of summer, you can dump without pain of death; but an unplanned swim is still a blow to the ego. So spring, summer, fall, or winter, the top of the river is the place any canoe traveler will choose to be.

But rivers have tops in a different sense, too; and the top of any river—meaning the place where it rises—has always held endless allure for me and for lots of other people who believe, as I do, that the river is not only our greatest metaphor for life but is the very stuff of life itself—the cold, wet feet; the warmth of the sun on your back; the tedium; the exhilaration; the beginning and the end; the unending flow. The source of anything as mighty and mysterious as all that has to be pretty mighty and mysterious itself, and indeed it is.

If you're not out hunting for trophy-sized metaphors or first causes, then the top of the river can simply be wherever you happen to put your canoe in, and the bottom is where you take out. It makes your life easier if you can think in those more modest terms, and much of the time I can. For a day trip on the Dead River, the top may be Spencer Rips. For an afternoon closer to home, I can get on the Sandy at Strong and float down the seven or eight miles to Farmington. And when the water is high in Temple Stream, which runs through my own land just fifty yards in back of the house, my own yard is the top. I can walk out my back door, plop my boat into the water, and have myself a wild little five-mile ride down to the mill pond in West Farmington.

But what pulls me irresistibly is the real top of the river, the source of the source, the top above which there is no other top; and sooner or later I'll go looking for the top of any river within my reach. For the ones I dream about but probably won't get to see, I do my scouting on the map. Theoretically, finding where a river rises should be pretty straightforward. You take a map, start at the river's mouth, and trace back on the main stem until you come to that pond or trickle that is farthest from the mouth. Easy, right?

No, not so easy. Even on a map, much less on the ground, the top of the river can be an elusive goal. Who could ever say what the headwaters of Labrador's Churchill River are? Where, in that labyrinth of lakes, rivers, and streams that covers the tableland of the Labrador-Quebec peninsula, is the most remote trickle that feeds the most remote pond that in turn flows into the Ashuanipi River, which in its turn flows from and into and out of how many hundred lakes before it reaches the Churchill? Lake Itasca in Minnesota is supposed to be the headwaters of the Mississippi, and there are lots of pictures of people shaking hands on its shores, pleased with themselves for having reached the source of America's Father of Waters. But if a river's *real* headwaters are those farthest from the river's mouth and at the greatest height above it, then aren't the headwaters of the Mississippi way over in western Montana where the Missouri rises?

Even our small, simple, down-home rivers in Maine offer some conundrums. If you want to be sloppy about it, I suppose you can call Chamberlain and Eagle and Churchill lakes the headwaters of the Allagash. But if you pole up Allagash Stream from Chamberlain to Allagash Lake, you're on an even headier headwater; and sticking out the far side of Allagash Lake is more of Allagash Stream; and if you go up *that*, you'll wind up at Allagash Pond, which is fed by some nameless little brooks that slide down the hillsides there. Chasing headwaters, you soon find out, is like chasing the last Quaker on the Quaker Oats box.

Last June, though, I'd had enough of this frustration, and I set out on a delicious summer afternoon determined to reach what I could finally and definitively call the headwaters of Temple Stream. If I couldn't find the top of this two-bit creek that runs through my own place and can't be more than fifteen miles long from one end to the other, how would I ever manage to find the source of the Yukon or the Mackenzie?

Trivial as this assignment may seem, it was not without its problems. Looking at the map, you'd have to call Schoolhouse Pond the source of Temple Stream because it is as far away from the confluence with the Sandy River as the stream goes. But there are a number of small feeder streams that are almost as long as the Schoolhouse Pond branch and rise at higher elevations. Height won out over distance in my definition of headwaters for that day, and I took an old twitch road up onto the slopes of Spruce Mountain.

At this level, the hillside was predominantly hardwoods, and as I made my way among leaves washed a nearly luminescent green by rains from the day before, the sound of the brook, still freshly charged with that rain, became louder and louder.

Good, I thought, I'll have more than a soggy ditch to follow up into the clouds.

The brook split into two branches where the road crossed it. I chose the right branch, and because I still haven't gone back to check out the left one, I can't tell you whether I chose the "correct" branch or whether the other would have taken me ten or twenty feet higher on the slope before it petered out. I can tell you, though, that walking up the branch I did choose took me to a place I had not expected to go. Following it up the hill was like watching a film of a child's life run backwards. At first, the brook was a noisy adolescent bounding down over mossy rocks, then a somewhat more tentative ten-year-old, still full of energy and curiosity but without that pubescent frenzy; farther still, it was a six-year-old perhaps, gentle, wide-eyed, padding along a leafy, meandering path where the reduced force and volume of the water were not strong enough to sweep the fallen leaves out of its way. And so I traced the brook back to its earliest infancy, finding tiny little dams of leaves and twigs that held no more than a saucepanful of water, clambering up over rocks where Temple Stream was no more than a trickle seeping down through a fissure.

Finally, as I came up onto a small plateau on the shoulder of the hill, there was no more water to be seen on the surface; but walking another thirty yards in a barely perceptible, elliptical depression in the ground I could feel the saturated soil beneath the leaf pack yielding under my feet. Then I was on dry land, and there was no place else to go but straight up into thin air, which is, of course, where the headwaters of Temple Stream and the Allagash and the Churchill and the Mississippi really are. The scientists call it the hydrologic cycle. But when I'm on a hilltop in western Maine and the late afternoon sun is slanting down through the spruce and maple of a little glen that is a gathering place of rainwaters for Temple Stream, which flows into the Sandy River, which flows into the Kennebec, which flows into the sea—well, then I call it a gift of heaven, a joy, a delight, a downright miracle.

Animal Spirits

Our new dog, Lucy, is a bird dog but not the kind you'll see on the cover of *Outdoor Life*. She will occasionally freeze into the Pointer's noble pose—right front paw lifted, nose stretched out, tail stiff and immobile—but pointing is not her preferred mode, and partridge and woodcock are not her preferred quarry. She is fondest of chickadees, and what she likes best to do is streak out the kitchen door like a black cannonball to chase a couple of them from the lilac bush by the porch into the big maple in the yard. Some frantic barking under the tree will soon dislodge the birds again, sending them down into the alders along Temple Stream with Lucy in hot pursuit. Then the birds fly back to the maple. And then back to the alders. I can't tell you precisely what is going on either in the bird brains or the dog brain, but everyone seems to be having a good time flying and running back and forth.

The dog certainly is. There may be some deep ethological explanation for why she is doing what she is doing, but from where I stand on the back porch it looks like she's just having some fun, which is the very best reason I know for doing anything.

We got Lucy from the Farmington animal shelter late last fall. She was on the outer edges of puppyhood then, maybe six or seven months old. What her lineage is I can only guess. She may have a dash of black Lab, but she stands only about nineteen inches high and hasn't the chunky build of a Lab. Except that she is all black, she looks like a scaled-down English Setter: a smooth, silky coat; fringed tail and leggings; ears long but not too long; domed head; a soulful eye.

I dote on her; she dotes on me. Doting may be intolerable between people—Rita tells me to get lost if I try it on her—but it's the perfect means of communication between dog and human. Lucy never tires of hearing how beautiful and brilliant she is, how exquisitely soft and silky her ears are, what a good dog she is. I never tire of telling her. She greets me, unfailingly, every morning with leaping, licking, squirming, dancing, tail-wagging, and her own special good-morning maneuver, which involves sliding her head down your leg until her forehead hits the floor, then somersaulting over onto her back to get her belly scratched.

What a revelation! A creature whose first act every day is a wild display of affection and whose second one is an invitation to play tug-of-war with an old sock. What a fine sense of priorities! I know as well as she does that love and play are what life is all about. But do I act on that knowledge every morning? No, I do not. I wake up thinking about the day's, the week's, the month's duties and obligations: this manuscript to finish, those telephone calls to make, that jag of wood to split, this fence to fix, that oil to change. Where I—poor human sod—shoulder my day and shrug into it like a heavy pack, her heart leaps up whether she beholds a rainbow in the sky or not.

She is named for Lucy in the Sky with Diamonds (not rainbows). And though she does not have kaleidoscope eyes, she helps me see much more of the world in far brighter color than I do on my own. As a member of one of nature's slowest and clumsiest species, I tend to seek out the easiest path to travel and, even if I'm out walking for pleasure, the most direct route between two points. Lucy is not troubled by such considerations. While I am traversing a steep hillside, she will race up and down it half a dozen times. She is my faster, more surefooted alter ego; and through her I come to know any landscape I travel far more intimately than I could otherwise. Following her with my eye, I can trace contours I haven't the time or speed to cover myself. With her feet, she expands my horizons. And as she travels, she not only telegraphs back to me the curves and crannies of the land, but also tells me, as she follows her nose, how many other creatures have passed through these same woods, leaving a maze of spoor behind them. For every set of tracks I may see, she scents out a dozen or two dozen or three dozen more. In the winter, if she comes across a set of moose tracks in deep snow, she'll stick her head down out of sight in each one, drinking in that moose perfume with great snuffing and whoofing. Now, on the bare ground of summertime, she'll race along, nose to earth, zigging and zagging with each fresh scent she picks up. She stops at this tree to sniff after the squirrel that climbed up it, at the top of that knoll to sort out the messages carried to her on the updraft. She reminds me of how much I miss and how much I don't understand, and I find that reminder both humbling and exhilarating.

Exhilarating, too, is my young dog's physical prowess, her speed and agility, her brute beauty and valor. If she were in the wild, those qualities would serve her well in pursuing her food and eluding her enemies. As it is, she can afford to put them in the service of play. She is an amazing broken-field runner. She romps often with a neighbor's large German-Shepherdly mutt who, on the straightaway, could probably outrun her. But in the game of chasing, wrestling, and chasing again, she literally runs circles around him. She feints, sprints, dodges, wipes her pursuer off against a tree. If he bowls her over with his greater weight, she rolls three times and comes up running. She clears obstacles with great soaring leaps that she will sometimes make just for the sheer delight of making them, whether anything is blocking her path or not. She seeks out big rocks, down trees, stone walls, and packed, frozen snowbanks—anything that will afford her a launching pad for a landlocked, canine swan dive.

Something in her wants to take to the air, and I sometimes wonder if her passion for birds isn't born of a yen to be airborne herself, if she too doesn't dream—as I do—of running, running, and suddenly feeling the grip of gravity fall away, of being able to take strides of six feet, then twelve and twenty-five, and finally of leaving the ground altogether to glide and soar and catch an updraft and glide a little farther still.

But the instant that thought crosses my mind I recognize it for the anthropomorphizing hokum it is. What constitutes Lucy's genius is that she does not dream herself different from what she is, that her spirit and flesh are truly one, that her own soaring leap is all she needs. If we attribute our feelings to animals, the injustice lies not so much in our falsely investing creatures simpler than ourselves with our complex psyches; rather, it is in demeaning that bright, clear animal spirit by cluttering it with the debris of our own.

Our distance from wild animals is usually so great that we are able only to learn about them, not from them. But dogs are our ambassadors from the animal world. Because they are willing to reside among us, interpreting the language of the wild into a language we can understand, they can show us how good it is to live life rather than worry about it. So when I go out with Lucy, I may try to train her a bit, but it's she who does most of the teaching.

November on
Maine 150

The high drama of autumn is over. The hillsides are no longer ablaze with color. No more busloads of leaf peepers cruise the byways of the north country. A couple of days of hard rain driven on a northeast wind have stripped maple, birch, and popple bare. The red oaks hang onto their dark brown leaves tenaciously, but wind and rain have taken their toll even of them, battering their crowns and leaving clumps of dark brown only on the lower, sheltered branches.

On the back roads, pickup trucks are pulled into turn-arounds and abandoned logging yards, and at dusk men in blaze-orange caps and sweatshirts emerge from the shadows of the woods to climb into the cabs and drive home.

Maine may sell some 36,000 non-resident hunting licenses a year, but here along Route 150 in the little towns of Athens, Harmony, and Cambridge, you can tell, even without looking at the plates on the trucks and weathered sedans, that these unhurried figures with the slightly bent but strong, stringy frames are not alien but native to this country of farms and woodland where innumerable small brooks thread their way between the hills and eventually make their way to the Kennebec, the Sebasticook, the Piscataquis.

This is the time of year when upcountry Maine and the people in it take a deep breath and let out a long sigh. The land is like a big dog, turning slowly around and around in the dry leaves before it settles down for a good nap, its nose tucked under its tail. The last fall chores remain to be done, but the pace is unhurried, the air soft and inviting one day, blustery and threatening the next.

I love Route 150 at any time of year, but now it has a special sweetness about it. It is a short highway as highways go, almost all of its fifty miles running from Skowhegan on the Kennebec to Guilford on the Piscataquis, with only the last twelve sticking up north of Guilford to end on the shores of Sebec Lake. So when you travel 150, you travel in a world unto itself, climbing gradually out of the Kennebec valley, dropping down again into tiny stream valleys, but then climbing again, always gaining altitude slightly, until from the height of land in Parkman just southwest of Guilford, you drop quickly and steeply into the Piscataquis valley, your traverse from one major watershed to another complete.

The first hints of that slow, rollercoaster ascent come

just after 150 leaves the flats of north Skowhegan with their jumble of modest homes and trailers. You can feel a slight lift in the terrain, as though your car were about to become airborne, and on the right, perched high on the first small hill to intrude into this flat land, is a proud old white farmhouse. The fields that have been mowed are still tinged with green, but the untended ones are rich with the subdued bouquets of fall—the deep browns of dead ferns, of meadowsweet, of goldenrod clusters gone to seed; the light tan, nearly wheat-colored leaves of swale grass; the white fluff of exploded milkweed pods; the red, green, brown, yellow medley of raspberry leaves.

On a knoll in Cornville where the Revere School Road comes in on the right and the Wood Road from the left, you can look across the fields to the western mountains. A gallery of huge sugar maples lines the Wood Road here, and behind a white rail fence stands a classic Maine Cape with a white brick chimney and a weathered gray barn. Off to the east, the hardwoods crown West Ridge with the silver-gray sheen of their bared limbs.

Straight as a string the road runs through the rest of Cornville, past huge fields, the yellow and brown of tamarack stands, Bruno Poulin's flourishing dairy farm. At Case Corner it jogs right, nips across the Athens line, and as you swoop into the outskirts of Athens village, the Church of the Open Bible greets you. Right next to it is a sign that says "Christ for the Lumberjack, Inc., Conference Grounds, Founded 1961."

The Conference Grounds are not hopping at this time of year, but on a glass-covered bulletin board under some big white pines in the yard, you can read this faded notice:

"Dear Friends,

"After much prayer and consideration, we believe that Our Lord is leading us to change the financial policy concerning the camp grounds.

"As you all know, we tried to carry on this ministry with love gifts from those who used the grounds and facilities. Dear ones, this has not worked. We have not been able to break even financially . . ."

Whereupon the schedule of fees for the pool, cabins, and tenting and trailer areas follows.

Athens, as the name would lead you to believe, is a village with many cultural and civic attributes; and I sometimes think that much of Route 150's appeal for me is, first of all, the presence of those two great cultural centers—Athens and Cambridge—and, secondly, the fact that they are linked by Harmony sandwiched in between them.

Across from the fairgrounds and gazebo in Athens is a big red barn with the sign "Redemtion Center" on it and all manner of truck piled up in the yard outside. At Christ for the Lumberjack, you can redeem your soul; at the Redemtion Center, you can redeem your bottles. And if you have more than nickel refunds on your mind, you can buy, sell, and trade there as well.

Around the corner, past Dee and Larry's Country Store, you're in the heart of downtown Athens. On your left, the town hall, L and L Enterprises, the Bush-Batcher Post 192 and Aux. of the American Legion, the Athens Fire Dept. The Bush-Batcher Post runs a Flea Market, starting August 13–14 and on every weekend thereafter until further notice. A faded, crayoned sign advises that "Anyone wishing to join the American Legion Post 192 or pay their dues may do so here!"

Across the road is Scott's Nation Wide Gen Mdse, now closed down, with the primal Coca-Cola signs on either side of the store's name: "Ice Cold, The Sign of Good Taste."

But all on Route 150 is not old-style, backcountry Maine. As you head north out of Athens village, you come upon inroads of the Brave New World—the Gorbell/Thermo Electron Power Co., for one, a new biomass power plant cranking out sixteen megawatts of electricity. And then the state highway department has been tinkering Route 150 itself from Athens clean through to the Guilford line, widening its shoulders, mellowing out its grades, repaving its surface, repainting its lines.

Alongside this road-fit-for-tourism, though, life has not changed that dramatically—yet. After Lord's Hill the road is dead straight again for about four miles of rolling country, and the human habitations and enterprises along this stretch are an index to the lives lived here and monuments to the Maine way of making do or doing without. There are some big old farms still run in the old way, well kept up, obviously solvent, but nothing fancy. And there are old farmhouses renovated with new money that positively drips off their eaves. There is the Harmony Small Engines Shop; a tiny, makeshift sawmill; Cotta's Country Curls, which, according to a sign in the vestibule of Carr's Store in Harmony village, offers Trimming, Tanning, and Toning and Invites You to a Free Demo on Our New Slenderizer Toning Tables and Total Body Massage Tables.

There are mobile homes and modest, FHA-financed

ranch houses with neat yards, a skidder, and two ATVs next to the garage. There are ancient, rusting trailers—not mobile homes at all—with one tar-papered addition sticking out in back and another sticking out in front. There are crumbling, low-roofed log camps. There is the burnt-out hulk of what was once a grand three-story farmhouse. There are nondescript little roadside houses atilt on rotting sills and still sporting the mud-colored asphalt siding sold to a small million rural New Englanders some forty or fifty years ago. The yards are crowded with rotting cars, wheel-less school buses, rusting woodstoves, old tub-style washing machines, light green, with four spindly legs and a wringer on top.

Again you climb and descend, this time into the notch where the houses of Cambridge nestle on the hillsides sloping down into Cambridge Pond. The road goes right across the dam that forms the pond, and the Grange hall, a tiny store, and perhaps the simplest monument I have ever seen mark the center of this spare little town. The stone is a rectangular slab with a plaque on it: "Dedicated to the Men and Women of Cambridge Who Served in the Wars of Our Country." Behind it, a flagpole; to either side, two small concrete urns with plastic flowers in them. And in one urn, the remains of an American flag, only the blue field and white stars fluttering in the fall breeze.

Now you head for the last and highest of Route 150's ridges, always this climbing and falling, but here the climbs are steeper and longer; and once you pass Parkman crossroads complete with its church, honor roll, and KC's Country Store, you hit French Hill and know you're climbing for real.

The top is wide open, and I always have to stop and

gawk. The westerly breeze on this overcast day is strong and cold up here. Ken Johnson's Jersey cows are sheltering in the lee of his aging, shingled barn, and an orange tarp covering a pile of hay bales is stretched out straight and snapping in the wind. Ken's tractors stand in front of the barn like tired horses—a red I-H with a bucket loader on it, a red Massey-Ferguson, a Case crawler for yarding wood. To the south and east, you can see forever out over Harlow Pond and the Sebasticook valley. The gray sky arches over the gray of the hardwood slopes, the green of the softwoods, the lighter green of mowed fields, the buffs and browns and tans. There it is, all of it spread out at your feet. And when you've stood and looked so long that the wind has cut through your clothes and yanked your shoulders up around your ears, you climb back into the car. You drop down into the Piscataquis valley, down into Guilford, down where people work in the mill, pump gas, go to school, down where this high, spare hillside seems not just five minutes but light years away.

Tumbledown Revisited

The plan for the day's outing was to ski from Rangeley to Weld. My friend Bill and I had been meaning to do it all winter. Now, at the end of February, there had already been some days of thaw and freeze, and we realized we'd better do it soon or winter would sneak away from us before we knew it.

Tumbledown was not on the itinerary, or only tangentially so. Among the cluster of hills and mountains that overlook Webb Lake to the west of Farmington and Wilton, Tumbledown is perhaps the most spectacular, taking its name from the sheer 700-foot cliffs on its south face. And on top, nestled into the saddle between Tumbledown and Little Jackson, is a small jewel of a mountain tarn.

But all that had no bearing on our plans. We were going on a cross-country ski tour, not a climbing trip. On its final leg we would skirt the base of Tumbledown, a fact I considered utterly irrelevant to the day's adventure. We'd gotton off in the gray hours of a gray morning, and having left Bill's car on the Byron Notch road where the Parker Ridge Trail to Tumbledown meets it (and as far in as the town had plowed), we had headed north to Rangeley.

As we had turned onto the road at Long Pond just east of Rangeley, Tumbledown, which was about twenty-five miles away, was the last thing on my mind. The first thing on my mind was whether I could ski even five miles, much less twenty-five, under what looked to be less than ideal conditions. On snowmobile trails the snow was packed hard and icy. Off the trails, it was crusty and scratchy. As for my own condition—well, I do a lot of skiing, but I don't bite off twenty-five miles every day. I knew I'd be just fine on good snow—comfortably tired at the end of the day with even a little extra energy left over. But on this crud? The night before I'd ironed a thin layer of blue klister onto my skis to handle the ice. If that turned out to be the wrong choice and we couldn't concoct any combination of waxes that would work really well, we might be facing a very long day of grunting and groaning.

But as we parked the car, a light snow started to fall, an unexpectedly fine, cold snow, so we rubbed on some green cake wax. That was our first pleasant surprise on a day that would turn out to be full of them. That combination of blue klister and green hard wax worked like a dream, and we sailed up the logging road on the east hip of Beaver Mountain as easily as if we were skiing on January's finest powder.

About two miles in, the road forks. If you bear left, you keep heading up the valley under Four Ponds Mountain until the logging road ends. You push over the height of land and then head down an old woods road past a bog and one of those tiny little forest ponds that appear, at best, like unpromising blue dots or squiggles on a map; but when you come upon them in reality, they seem like oases of the soul, places where you want to pitch your tent and do nothing but watch the sun come up and go down, casting morning and evening shadows of spruce and fir across the immaculate surface of the snow.

In another five minutes we were at Sabbathday Pond, about sixty acres of crystal-clear trout water where, under a drizzly, windy September sky that felt meaner and colder than this February one, I'd spent a day trying to lure one last trout of the year out of that gray, choppy water. Unsuccessful, I'd then wallowed my way back to the Appalachian Trail on the marshy road along the east shore. Now we skimmed along that same soggy, hummocky old logging road as if it were greased; and once past the pond we began one of those long downhill runs that are neither too flat nor too steep and that give an earthbound cross-country skier some idea of what it must be like to soar and swoop on hawk's wings. Almost three miles we glided from Sabbathday down along Welch Brook until we hit the main stem of the Swift River and our glory ride was over.

The Swift River isn't really a river at this point. It's more a large brook, but here in these hills it is every bit as swift as it is downstream from Byron to Mexico where it gives spring canoeists one of western Maine's wildest rides. As we turned north to make the gradual, three-mile ascent along the stream toward the Swift's headwaters, the sun broke out; and when it was time for lunch, we cradled ourselves comfortably in the branches of some down trees, ate our sandwiches and oranges, and let the sun massage us almost to sleep.

If the first half of this trip is lovely, the second half is exquisite. Leaving the valley of the Swift's main branch, the trail climbs easily through big hardwoods that have never seen the likes of a skidder or chain saw. Then, on a narrow woods track that predates mechanized logging, it drops down into the valley of the Swift River's East Branch and follows that waterway down to the Byron Notch road, giving skiers their second long soaring run of the day.

When Bill and I were about two-thirds of the way down, the sun gave way not only to clouds again but to a snow squall. I'd been skiing bare-handed and with just a light wool shirt on. Now I needed another layer of wool, mittens, and a rain suit over the whole business, and I wished I had the goggles I'd forgotten to put in my pack. The snow was so thick that it stung the eyes no matter how we squinted against it, and we were soon plastered with it, looking like two mobile snowmen.

But when we came onto the lower stretch of road where it rolls up and down over the lower spurs of Dolly Mountain and where the bulldozers have been at work again, the squall was over as quickly as it had begun. The white bell jar that had kept us from seeing twenty-five yards ahead of us was suddenly lifted, and from the knoll we were on, we could see Tumbledown breaking free from the clouds, too. Barely two miles away, it seemed to tower over us; and, from this vantage point in the west, the steep face that gives it its name seemed nearly perpendicular, far grander and steeper and fiercer and nobler than it does from the east, which is the direction I almost always approach it from, the direction from which it had become familiar as an old shoe.

Tumbledown, with its measly 3,068 feet, is a far cry from Nanga Parbat or Everest or K-2 or even from many of our more modest Rocky Mountains. But on that afternoon, as the clearing wind drove the clouds away from it into a deep blue sky and the sun, low on the horizon, flooded Tumbledown's green and granite and snow with light, I didn't think there was a mountain in the world that could have given me as much pleasure as this old friend I had hardly expected to see at all on this trip but was now seeing with new eyes.

When Tumbledown burst out of the snow clouds that afternoon, I suddenly realized that I'd gotten a bit blasé about Tumbledown over the years, not jaded but certainly blasé. I'd been up and down it so many times over so many years with so many people at so many different times of the year that it had begun to feel about like my own woodlot: a place I always enjoy going to but one that provides pleasures like those of variations on a theme in music—the familiar seen in a new light but not a dramatically new one. The response is one of mellow appreciation, not "Wow! I mean like really WOW!"

But now, without even setting foot on Tumbledown, it had come to me literally out of the blue, smiting me with all the force of fresh infatuation. And as the wind out of the west grew in strength and practically blew us back to the car, sending us skimming along like animated iceboats on the wide hardpack of the Byron Notch road, I found myself thinking of old Heraclitus and his paradoxes about the shiftiness of all that is permanent and the permanence of all that is shifty. "Nothing endures but change," he said. And: "It is not possible to step into the same river twice." I would add a corollary or two: You never climb the same mountain twice. You never even *see* the same mountain twice. Most of the time I forget that. Most of the time when I climb or see Tumbledown I think it's the same Tumbledown I climbed or saw before. But now I'll try to remember that the only man who sees the same mountain twice is a man who hasn't been looking.

Machines, Accursed and Wondrous

The distinction is easy to make: We love machines when they work and hate them when they don't. We love the lawnmower that mows, the baler that bales, the chain saw that saws. We love the family car that starts up cheerfully at fifteen below zero, and we hate its metallic guts when it strands us on the New Jersey Turnpike on a steamy July afternoon.

Not everyone has this love-hate relationship with machines. My friend Jack, for example, can keep his head around machinery no matter how badly it mistreats him. When his baler has spit out its third or fourth gnawed mass of hay and twine, Jack will calmly climb down from his tractor, shut off the baler motor, and say, "Well, now, let's have us a little look-see here." He remains unruffled. He understands that some crucial part is worn or broken, that some crucial adjustment has become maladjusted. Something that is within his powers to cope with needs his attention.

Jack's view of machinery is utilitarian. Machines are tools, just as a hammer is a tool. If you break a hammer handle, the diagnosis and the treatment are simple. You see instantly what is wrong, and you replace the broken handle. A fancy four-wheel drive diesel tractor with a high range and a low range and eighteen speeds forward and backward and hydraulic ups and downs is a tool, too. If it quits and lies down on the job, your problem may be more complex than with the hammer, but in principle it is just the same. The tool is broken, and all you have to do is fix it. That's the way Jack looks at machines. He neither loves nor hates them. For him, they are just more or less complicated hammers.

My own view of machines is a demonic one. Somewhere on the spectrum between the hammer and a Hewlett Packard mainframe, tools cease to be mere tools. They become animate beings. They can be wooed, placated, flattered, coaxed. Sometimes they will do what we ask of them, sometimes not. In a matter of seconds a machine that is the image of cooperation, patience, and docility can turn nasty, stubborn, even vindictive. If machines really were mere soulless tools, then why is it—when the temperature is right around freezing and a mixture of snow and rain is pelting down out of the November sky and when I finally realize that it's a rotten day for cutting firewood and I head for home with my last twitch of logs—why is it that my ancient little Cletrac crawler

130

decides just halfway through the only mud wallow in the trail that this is the perfect time to lie down and take a nap? Why just now? Why in just this godawful place?

Vengeance, that's why. The little beast didn't want to come out at all today, and now he's getting back at me. I can stand knee-deep in icy mud and crank my arm off.

"Too bad, Buster," Cletrac says, "I ain't a-gonna be treated thisaway."

"Now, listen," I say, "be reasonable. Who has oiled and greased and fueled you all these years? Who has tinkered you and bought you new parts when you needed them and loved you like a brother?"

"Stop it. You bring tears to my headlights."

"You don't have any headlights."

"See what I mean? Gross negligence. Flagrant tractor abuse."

"But you never have to be out at night, never."

"You think I wouldn't enjoy a little night life now and then? I can't remember the last time I took in a movie. Work, work, work, that's all you want me for."

"I'll try to be a little more considerate. Now, how about getting us home? Wouldn't you rather spend the night in your nice dry shed instead of out here in this slop?"

"It's all one to me. I'm cold-blooded."

Along about this point I start screaming, ranting, and jumping up and down (as best one can jump in mud). I may even make the fatal mistake of whacking Cletrac a sharp blow alongside the head. That is the ultimate humiliation. He clams up completely now; and, crank as I will, I can't raise even an encouraging burble from him. It will probably cost me a new set of points and plugs to get back in his good graces.

On my hammer-to-computer scale, the Cletrac occupies a place just over the line into the demonic, which is to say it is inhabited by a demon of a low-enough, domesticated-enough variety that even someone with my limited training and experience in demonology can get on with him, most of the time, and, indeed, even grow fond of him. My Cletrac is an ancient machine—a tractor primeval—older than I and all bone and muscle. It is little more than a steel frame on tracks with an engine and clutch in front, a transmission, differential, and power take-off slung on behind. And that bare minimum is quite enough.

If I take a close look at the few machines that occupy a special place in my life and try to pin down just what it is about them that inspires infatuation, I find that with one notable exception (my word processor) they are all old and they all display great simplicity in design and function. In many machines built prior to World War II, their descent from hand tools is still quite obvious. The connection between the machine and the job it is meant to perform is clear at first glance. When men first attempted to fly, they did not build jet fighters. They manufactured artificial bird wings, strapped the wings onto their arms, then jumped off a high wall, flapping wildly. Early horse-drawn farm machinery showed this same clear lineage. A hay rake, after all, was nothing more than an oversized hand rake hung between wheels and equipped with a trip to dump the hay. An early mowing machine was nothing more than a bunch of double-edged blades mounted on a bar and driven back and forth by an eccentric geared to the turning axle of the mower. Simple. No demons had entered the scene yet. Those machines—like the lever, the inclined plane, and the block and tackle—did nothing but multiply our animal powers somewhat. The gains were not so great as to inspire hubris.

I don't know in exactly which year the Cletrac was built, but I do know they don't build them that way anymore. It is the only one of my '30s-vintage machines still extant today, and it positively drips nostalgia for me. I ran it on and off for fifteen summers hauling firewood for my father's sporting camps in northern Maine. Then, when he sold his camps, I trucked the Cletrac down to Temple, where it has hauled my firewood for another seventeen years. It has been a faithful, if sometimes balky, companion of my whole adult life.

Whatever faults it may have, it cannot be accused of deviousness. Everything about it is straightforward and up front. It has no fuel pump, for example. Gravity draws the gas from the fuel tank to the carburetor. Nor does it have a battery, generator, alternator, or voltage regulator. Instead, it has a magneto with four lead wires to the four spark plugs. In place of a starter, there is a hand crank. The crank is my direct line to Cletrac's heart. If he's in good spirits, all I have to do is wind on that crank a few times, and off he'll go.

Inside, he has four cylinders lined up in a straight row. That seems to me the only decent number of cylinders and the only decent arrangement for them that an engine should have. I can grasp how a straight four works; I know that when piston number one is on its power stroke, piston two is compressing, four is intaking, and three is exhausting. If I stretch my imagination about as far as it can go, I can even figure out what each of Cletrac's eight valves should be doing anywhere in that cycle. But where any one of sixteen valves will be in a V-8, that I do not know, and I don't think I even want to know.

Cletrac has nothing to hide. Walk around him once, and you've seen everything there is to see. It's nice to have socket wrenches to work on him, but he's so open to the world that you can do just about anything you need to do with open ends, box heads, a screwdriver, and a pair of pliers. You put the gas in here, the oil in there, the anti-freeze up here. You turn that crank to get going; you pull this lever to go left, that one to go right. Simple is what he is. With him there's A and B and C. There's no Aa or Bb(1) or abba.

The steam locomotive is traditionally referred to as the "iron horse," but that's a misnomer. My Cletrac is a true iron horse because he needs no rails to run on. He's not as tall as a Percheron, but he's otherwise everything we could ask of an iron horse: big enough to haul one big tree or two medium-sized ones or a bundle of small stuff; small enough to squirm around in the woods without squashing the whole world flat; simple enough that my four-cylinder mind can maintain him and repair him without any spe-cialized knowledge or specialized tools.

The Cletrac's dimensions are human. It is much stron-ger than I am but not so much stronger that its very presence in the woods is a disaster. Unlike a skidder, it does not destroy everything in its path in the process of hauling out a few logs. You can see where it has been, but it does not leave carnage behind it. Whoever built the Cletrac had a wonderful sense of proportion.

MACHINES, ACCURSED AND WONDROUS

No one is going to build Cletracs or Model A Fords again, but I would hope that today's and tomorrow's engineers might take an occasional look back at them as models of simplicity and proportion, which is to say, as machines whose demons are by and large benign and altogether deserving of the affection we feel for them.

Living on the Edge

Eliza Snook lived in Stokes State Forest, and both Eliza and that forest played a large part in my formative years. Stokes State Forest is in the northwesternmost tip of New Jersey, snuggled up against the Pennsylvania and New York borders. It is in the Kittatinny Mountains, which are very small as mountains go; the Flat Brook, which is not much of a trout stream as trout streams go, flows through it; and as state or national or provincial parks and forests go, Stokes is pretty small potatoes, too. But for me, a suburban New Jersey kid, it was the essence of wilderness, of paradise. There were woods and fields and brooks and ponds near my home; but, much as I roamed them and loved them, they lacked something that

Stokes had: They were not inviolable. Even as a boy whose experience did not include the overnight destruction of cherished landscapes, I sensed that any land not expressly put aside and preserved as it was would sooner or later give way to housing developments, streets, streetlights, the buzz of lawnmowers on Saturday afternoons. And, indeed, it did.

But at Stokes, my family's favorite campsite, which was, as I recall, Number Three, would always be there on the banks of Stony Brook. And about fifty yards upstream there would always be a ledge where the water slithered down over the rock into a small pool, and from there I could always fish my way up to the pond where the Girl Scout camp was and where I had seen my father catch a pound-and-a-half trout off the dock.

And even if the Flat Brook cannot be numbered among world-class trout streams, it remains, in my mind, the trout stream primeval, the place where the magic of working riffles and pools took hold of me for all time, the pressure of moving water against my legs, the airy swarm of a mayfly hatch, a trout rising to a deftly placed Light Cahill. I carry a dream image of trout fishing around with me, and though I know I could never go back to the exact scene of that dream, I know it is somewhere on the Flat Brook.

Eliza and all the other Snooks had somehow managed to retain an enclave inside the forest. They lived *right in it* and were therefore—like elves and gnomes and trolls—different from us mere mortals. They had an existence far grander, larger, more mysterious than the rest of us, who lived on tiny plots of ground measured and marked off

137

and recorded in a Registry of Deeds. I envied the Snooks and was terrified of them. Never mind that their places were as duly registered as anybody else's. For me, they were as much a part of the forest as the rocks and the trees. They, too, were inviolable; and though Eliza was—in my boy's eyes—at least a hundred and twelve years old when I first encountered her, I suspect she is still in her little house on the Flat Brook yet; and if I went fishing through under the little bridge tomorrow, she would come hobbling out, bent over almost double, her face all hooked nose and prong chin and no teeth and long looping hairs growing out of her moles; and she would stand on the bridge to cast her evil eye on me as long as I was in sight. People who lived in immortal forests, I learned from her, were immortal themselves, creatures so much a part of the endless life cycles of their surroundings that they too would go on forever.

I've never been conscious of those early experiences bearing on my decisions in later life, but it just so happens that state and national parks have been major way stations for me, and that I now live not in Maine's Mount Blue State Park but on the borders of it. Mount Blue, at only 3,187 feet, is a modest mountain by any accounts; but it is a monument that emanates peace and even a touch of majesty into the landscape around it. When I drive Route 43 from Farmington to my home in Temple, a route I do drive several times each week, I head right for the mountain. In the winter, it is often crisp and clear and smack in front of me in the clean air. In July, it draws back into the summer haze and takes on that deep, purplish blue of its name.

I see it from many other places, too. From Allen's Pinnacle in Freeman, from Miles Square Road in Avon, from Webb Lake in Weld, from Day Mountain in Strong. Just about anywhere I go in this country on foot or on skis or snowshoes it will pop its head up. In its smaller way, Mount Blue and its park are to this area what Katahdin and Baxter State Park are to northern Maine. Where can you see Katahdin from? From just about everywhere. From Route 11 in the east and from Chamberlain Lake and Chesuncook in the northwest and from the state lunch site on South Twin Lake and from any old hill you care to bushwhack to the top of, north, south, east, or west.

Only a few weeks ago I camped on Lone Pine Point on Pemadumcook Lake, due south of the park, and there was all of Katahdin spread out in front of me, not just Baxter Peak and the Knife Edge, but the whole range, east to west, from Pamola on over to Doubletop. Then, the next day, my buddy and I paddled and poled and tracked our canoe up the Penobscot, and the mountain grew larger and larger in front of us, until, at Debsconeag Deadwater, it filled the whole northern horizon.

You don't have to spend too much time in Katahdin country to understand why Percival Baxter wanted to draw a line around the mountain and say, "This place we will leave alone for all time." Katahdin is a beacon that can guide us physically, geographically: If you can see the mountain, you know where you are. But, like the Grand Tetons or the Grand Canyon, it is also a beacon for the spirit, reminding us in language that brooks no backtalk that earth is our mother and our grave, our beginning and our end, that we owe her affection, respect, awe, and loving care.

139

UPCOUNTRY

In a less imposing voice but in no less moving tones, "my" little Mount Blue State Park tells me these same things; and I am grateful that the fates and my own inchoate ramblings have led me to a place where the forces of the earth spoke so powerfully to people before me that they declared this land to be the treasure it is. To live in or near a park, then, means more than just having at your doorstep a lovely reach of land that is as safe as land in our world can be. It also means remaining perpetually in touch with the spell of flowing water, of the mountain, of the raven's call, and so, like Eliza Snook, becoming something of an elf, a gnome, and a timeless troll oneself.

The Black-Fly Baron
of Franklin County

Experiments using the biological insecticide Bti to rid tourist areas of mosquitoes and black flies have been underway in Maine for some years now. While operators of golf courses and commercial campgrounds may greet these developments with glee, there are other groups who are less than enthusiastic. Fishermen, for example, know that black-fly larvae are a major food source for young trout and for the stoneflies and caddisflies on which trout and landlocked salmon feed. In northern Franklin County, allies of the fly have already formed a non-profit organization called Save Our Black Fly (SOB). John Sheridan of Stratton, the group's treasurer, says that many of SOB's supporters are veterans of SMOOSA (Save Maine's One and Only State Animal), the group that launched the un-successful referendum to make moose hunting illegal in Maine. "Most of these folks aren't even fly fishers," Sheri-dan says. "I guess they just figure since they failed to protect the state animal they're going to do their damned-est to protect the state bird."

Sheridan, who teaches biology at Langtown High School, might be open to the charge that his behavior is less than scientific and that he is setting a poor role model for his students. After all, there is as yet no air-tight scien-tific evidence that Bti is harmful to fisheries. "That may be," Sheridan says, "but I guess I'm going on the theory—which has been proved over and over again in other cases—that the components of an ecosystem are like the links in a chain. If you destroy one link, you destroy the chain."

I ask Sheridan why he is willing to be known as a figurehead in SOB when so many of the organization's members choose to remain anonymous. "I've got nothing to lose," he says. "But let the word get out among the business types that old Charley or Joe doesn't want to sacrifice black flies to the almighty tourist dollar, and he'll be finished. He'll be drummed out of the Rotary Club. That isn't to say we don't have quite a few sub rosa members from the business community. You know what I mean—stalwart members of the Western Maine Chamber of Commerce by day, and SOBs by night."

As we continue to talk about the place of the black fly in Maine life, it becomes clear that Sheridan's concern is not solely an environmental one but a sentimental one as well. "There's Katahdin, Moosehead Lake, the rock-bound

142

coast, and the Allagash. And there's the black fly. The flies are as much a part of our heritage as any of our great natural monuments. They're one of the things that makes Maine *Maine*. Take 'em away, and we'll be the poorer for it."

Sheridan is obviously devoted to his cause, but he does not claim to be the hardest of SOB's hard core. When I ask him who is, he motions me into his jeep; and after half an hour's drive on the paved road we go jouncing off over twelve miles of dirt road into a remote corner of western Maine's already remote backcountry.

The road ends in the dooryard of the most shipshape homestead I've ever seen. The house is a two-story log building, which, though clearly not new, wears none of that crumbling grunge that so many owner-built homes of the late sixties and early seventies seem to exude. The roof is of freshly painted standing-seam metal. The chinking is tight; the screen door is solid and fits snugly. Across the dooryard from the house is another large log building that serves as barn, workshop, garage, and toolshed. And beyond both buildings is a garden and perhaps four acres of open field where two goats are grazing.

"Used to be an old logging farm," Sheridan says. "Vern has been pushing the brush back a little bit more each year."

Vern Fulsom is sitting on the front steps of his house, sipping at a pint of home brew. He is not a big man, no more than five-foot-nine, but he is compact and muscular with no belly hanging over his belt despite the heavy dusting of gray in his black hair.

"I ain't exactly unfriendly," Fulsom says, handing us

143

each a pint bottle, "but like you can see, I want plenty of elbow room, and I figure where there's a high population of black flies there'll be a low population of human beings."

So Fulsom's main reason for protecting the black fly is to protect Maine from overdevelopment?

"That's about the size of it," Fulsom says. "It's the flies that separates the sheep from the goats. And in case you're missin' my point," he adds, his gray eyes narrowing down to steely slits, "it's the flies that separates the folks fit to live here year 'round from the goddam tourists. You know what some Audubon-type fella told me once? He said that if it wasn't for the flies, there'd be three times as many fishermen on our streams in June as there are now. Can you imagine? Some o' them yo-yos down to the State House in Augusta actually think that would be good."

When we've finished our beer, Fulsom leads us back past the goat pasture and into the woods where we can hear the rush of a small stream. Fulsom's youngest children—two dark-haired, snappy-eyed little girls of about six and eight whom Fulsom fondly calls Muggy and Buggy—have joined us. When we rose from our seats on the front steps, the girls had come tumbling out of the front door.

"Hey, Daddy," they asked, "ya gonna show him the bug farm? Can we come, huh?"

Back in the woods, we come upon five peculiar structures that look like long, serpentine quonset huts made of fine nylon mesh. They stand about seven feet high and are not much wider at the base, and I quickly realize that they are built as they are in order to arch over the small stream

144

and follow its twisting course. Inside them are millions upon billions of black flies.

"Get it?" Fulsom grins. "If they kill 'em off, we put 'em back."

"Buggy stuck her hand in a cage once," Muggy tells us, her eyes bugging wide, "and it came out ALL BLOODY."

"We can put 'em anywhere we want," Fulsom says. "We draw 'em off into big cages that are made of nothin' but wire and netting. A man can handle 'em easy as pickin' up a balloon. Then we load 'em into a truck, and we're off." Fulsom chuckles. "Can't you see it now? One of them golfy fellas linin' up a thirty-five-foot putt and gettin' himself all sniggled into position and wavin' his stick at the ball and then WHAMMO! A bubble full of my little babies hits him. The great thing about black flies is that they're much quieter than mosquitoes. They sneak up without warning. Him and his little putter will be black with them suckers."

Muggy and Buggy clap their hands and jump up and down, giggling wildly.

Sheridan, who has been letting Fulsom do all the talking until now, does a little smiling himself. Then, as we start heading back to Fulsom's place, he says, "We scientists in SOB are trying to breed a frost-resistant strain of *Simulium venustum* and see if we can't extend the season a bit. I do some downhill skiing myself, and the slopes are getting a little too crowded for my tastes. It'd be nice to thin things out, don't you think?"

"Yup," Fulsom says, looking out onto wooded hills with not a house in sight, "it's the black fly keeps us honest in this friggin' country; and if the black fly goes, then by the Jesus I go, too."

A Love Affair
with Drury Pond

A swim in the late afternoon just before supper is not a necessity of life, but it has become so much a part of our summer rhythm and ritual that any day we miss out on it feels curiously incomplete, a day not totally misspent, perhaps, but certainly one on which the circle has not been closed, the final chord not sounded.

Drury Pond is less than a mile away, and about five o'clock, bathing-suited and with towels slung over our shoulders, we climb into the car. We are usually four: Rita and I, our son, Greg, and our dog, Lucy. Lucy has neither bathing suit nor towel, but she does have some retriever blood in her, some streak of spaniel or Lab or both, and the prospect of her day's swim has her bouncing up and down like a black, floppy-eared yo-yo.

A LOVE AFFAIR WITH DRURY POND

Although we swim on all kinds of days—breezy days, misty days, overcast days—my image of the quintessential summer swim is one of a windstill July afternoon, of dead calm, of glassy, silent water, of the sun poised hot and glowing as a branding iron in the western sky. Away from the water, the heat is heavy and oppressive, weighing down on the shoulders, but as we walk down the shaded, pine-needled path to the pond, that weight lifts.

Lucy is always the first one in. Before we can kick off our sneakers and drop shirts and towels on the grass, she has gone flying off the end of the little floating pier. She swims in circles, snorting and chuffing to blow the water out of her nose, wondering what's taking us so long. Then we follow her, each in his or her own style. First, me with a flat dive; Greg with a running cannonball; Rita with considered caution. She sits on the end of the dock, dangling her legs in, getting acclimated. Then she slides in slowly, uttering vocalizations appropriate to the season, groans and gasps for the cold water of June and September, little sounds of appreciation for the cooling but not-too-cool temperatures of midsummer.

Drury is a small pond about half a mile long and hardly two hundred yards across here at its widest point. When we are out in the middle, we can see almost the whole shoreline. Right ahead of us, bordering a third of the east shore and hooking around the southern and outlet end of the pond, is a broad wetland where redwings flit among the reeds and where our splashing approach sometimes sends a great blue heron pumping up into the sky on its huge wings. At the north end is another bog where the inlet stream meanders into the pond. These wetlands and the steep hillsides that form much of the shoreline have discouraged extensive development, and the few summer camps here are a modest presence, not an arrogant intrusion, on the land. Beyond the bog, a hill too low and unexceptional to have a name rises gracefully from the valley floor, its flanks a rich, dark green in their late summer foliage; and still farther off, a couple of miles to the south, are the ledges and the softwood dome of Derby Mountain.

The view from the middle of Drury Pond is not one of high drama, not a grand, adventuresome vista. Unlike large lakes that lure the eye and the spirit out to the horizon and up to the huge, overarching blue of the sky, Drury Pond cuts off the long view and brings what is close to home into focus. Tucked away as it is down in the valley, it never lets you see the sky without seeing the hills reaching up into it. Heaven and earth are as intertwined here as sea and land are on the Maine coast. And on days like this, when the water is calm, we sometimes stop in the middle, tread water, take a few minutes to frolic and gab and rejoice in where we are and in our own good company. Greg does a few whale dives, his feet waving in the air like toed flukes before they slip under. Our talk is not intricate or brilliant. Like the ritual of the swim itself, it tends to be repetitive and celebratory. "I love this pond," Rita says. "I just love it." Or I may roll over on my back and float, all awash in the water and the heat of the sun, and say something incisive, like: "Ahhh! Oh, yeah. Mmmmm."

Lucy, impatient with our dawdling and tired of swimming circles around us, heads for the far shore, the widening arrowhead of her wake aimed straight at the little pine-studded headland we have christened Lucy Point because she insists on visiting it every day. Our own routine calls for swimming straight across the pond to touch a lily pad in the big raft of them along the bog. Then we swim up the shore to Lucy Point, turn, and angle back to the dock. Not one to be caught in the rear guard, Lucy comes racing out of the woods, plows up a great geyser of spray as she hits the water, and is soon out in front of the pack despite our head start on her.

Once again the circuit is complete: across the pond to the lily pads, up the shore to Lucy Point, then back to the start, about half a mile altogether. And as we towel off and Lucy makes a last splashing dash along the shore in pursuit of a kingfisher, I realize again, as I often have before, what a powerful grip this little pond has on me and how totally out of proportion to its "objective" value my affection for it is. I suspect that if the State Planning Office undertook an evaluation of lakes and ponds in organized townships, Drury Pond would rank quite low on the list. Its yellow perch and sunfish and pickerel hardly make it an outstanding fishery, nor would its modest, low-key loveliness win it high marks on a Watershed Aesthetics Survey. But no matter how well-intentioned such a study might be, it would miss what matters most, which is that people do not love a pond or river or landscape because it has been appraised and found valuable. They love it because their lives are intertwined with it, because they have seen it day after day, year after year, in sun, rain, and snow, because it is rich with memories of work and fun, of family and friends.

So when we go to Drury Pond for a swim on July

afternoons, we enjoy much more than the expected benefits. True, we get half an hour of the best whole-body
exercise there is. True, we wash off the sweat and grime of
the workday and come out refreshed and revived. But in
the mirror image of clouds, big pines, and the familiar
contours of Temple's hills reflected on the glassy surface
of the pond, we also see a distillate both of the beauty of
this place and of the lives we have lived here. Better still,
we aren't limited to just looking. We can jump right in and
splash around. In Drury Pond, we are immersed and
awash in what backcountry life in Maine is all about.

No wonder we hate to miss a day.

Cleaning Out
the Ell

Spring and fall up here in the hill country of western Maine always inspire me to clean out the ell. I am inspired in the fall because I know that in a few weeks it will be bitterly cold out in the ell—every bit as cold as outdoors but minus the wind—and I will not want to be pawing around in the family junk at subzero temperatures. Furthermore, having looked at this mess all summer, I can't bear to look at it all winter, too.

In the spring I am inspired because I know that in a few weeks it will be hellishly hot out there in the ell—every bit as hot as outdoors but with no air moving at all—and I will not want to be pawing around in the family junk in the stifling heat. Furthermore, I'm so sick of looking at the mess that was there all winter that I can't bear to look at it again all summer.

Why is it, then, if I am so powerfully motivated to beautify the ell, that a spring passes and then a fall and then still another spring and another fall and the ell is still not cleaned up and straightend out? Why, if anything, does it have a little more junk in it now, a couple of weeks before Thanksgiving, than it did when I attacked it last April?

I set about the task with a ruthless attitude adopted from an efficient, orderly friend of mine who lives in Queens (and who, mind you, has never had to cope with a Maine ell). Any item you have not used for two years, he said, you get rid of. Sell it, give it away, throw it away, it doesn't matter. Just get rid of it.

Wonderful. What could be clearer or simpler than that? I start upstairs in the ell, and the first thing my eye hits on is a parachute. I have not used it for two years. In fact, I have never used it, at least not for jumping out of airplanes. It came into my hands eighteen years ago in February when a young Air Force sergeant knocked on the door and asked if he could spread this parachute out in our back field. His unit was practicing search-and-rescue operations. The training planes were to fly over this part of the state and see if they could spot several parachutes scattered about the region.

"Sure," I said. "Will you come pick it up when your exercises are over?"

"No, it's not one that's safe to use anymore. Just leave it there for a week and then keep it. Old parachutes make great play tents for the kids."

The sergeant was right. In his preschool years, Greg and

his friends did use the chute a few times for a tent, and we even used it ourselves once for several months as a make-shift ceiling in a partially renovated room.

But why am I keeping it now? All our ceilings are long since finished. Greg has outgrown play tents. Surely, I'm not keeping it for our grandchildren. Or am I? Nonsense. Get rid of the silly thing. So I pick it up and start to toss it on the throw-out pile. But once it is in my hands, I start to admire it. A parachute is quite a lovely, intricate thing with its spiderweb of lines and its panels made of a smooth, shiny, tough nylon, some white and some blaze orange so the search-and-rescue teams can spot them against the snow.

No, even a retired parachute should not go to the dump, particularly not one that has served us as play tent and makeshift ceiling and that came here in the hands of a nice young guy whose face I still remember, and so I put the parachute on the hold-for-future-disposition pile.

Next is an old Remington office-style typewriter, vin-tage about 1908. The carriage floats around unhitched, but I am convinced that flaw can be repaired easily, and I know that one of these days all the generating facilities in the world will come to a grinding halt and there will be no more electricity to run our fancy computers and electric typewriters. That old machine will come in handy again someday. Besides, my father used it for years at Jim Pond, and I can still see it on the old roll-top desk in his camp.

And then there is the treadle sewing machine that will prove equally invaluable when the Big Switch is finally turned off for good and we're thrown back on our own muscle and Yankee ingenuity again. Not to mention the butter churn we used for a few years in our days of purer self-sufficiency and will no doubt return to when the flow of butter trucks from Wisconsin and Minnesota dries up.

And everybody who has a garden needs lots of canning jars, maybe not four long shelves three deep with them, but you never know. We may have a bumper crop of tomatoes. And even though I don't make beer myself, Jim Logan up in Strong can use those two cases full of old brown pint-size Narragansett bottles. I must remember to take them up to him.

What about this tin that once contained five pounds of Sunbeam Breakfast Cocoa? Well, it reminds me that at one time tinsmiths made cocoa containers. They soldered the joints and put a hinged lid on, and when you bought cocoa you also bought a handsome tin box you could use in your kitchen or workshop for another fifty years.

And so it dawns on me once again: I can't throw anything away because I really don't have any junk. Everything I lay my hands on up here is *good stuff*. I may not have any immediate use for it and may not have used it for years, but that doesn't mean that I or someone else may not have a use for it tomorrow. That is the article of faith that fuels all yard sales, and in its light there is hardly anything humble enough to be beyond resurrection. When we bought this house nearly twenty years ago, we found an old jeans jacket that Dana Hamlin, who had lived here for nearly seventy years, had left hanging in the ell privy. The privy is no longer a privy, but we saw no pressing reason to remove Dana's jacket. It caught Greg's eye a few weeks ago. He peeled the cobwebs out of it, washed it, and has since made it part of his funky wardrobe.

I can't say whether the cultural constellation that makes

this sort of thing possible is peculiar to rural Maine or not, but I know that if Greg had grown up in suburban New Jersey, as I did, there would have been no ell in which an old farmer's jacket could have waited—and been tolerated—until someone the age of Dana's great-grandson came along to claim it. Without the architectural institution of the ell, the symbiosis between junk and ell could never have developed. Junk, like a gas, expands to fill completely any container into which it is put, and the ell is the container just made for it to fill. So intimately linked are they that I often wonder which came first. Did a Yankee farmer, overwhelmed by the collection of stuff he had left lying outside as he passed back and forth from barn to house, decide to roof the heap over and close it in, hence inventing the first ell? Or did he build the ell so he could have an indoor privy and a sheltered passageway to the barn and discover only later that the ell's true destiny was to fill up with junk?

Add to the ell-junk symbiosis that combination of sentimentality, frugality, practicality, and pessimism so characteristic of the Yankee mind (or the rural mind or the human mind?), and you have the explanation for the state of my ell. I keep my butter churn and my horse-drawn hay rake because I'm fond of them, I know they've got to be worth quite a pretty penny, they work, and I can fall back on them when all these newfangled, lazy-man's electric and gas contraptions wind up on the junk heap where they belong.

So if you're in the market for a 1908 typewriter or a used parachute, you know where to look. But don't expect to walk away with them cheap.

Bringing Home
the Tree

We cut our tree on the Saturday before Christmas—late, I suppose, by most people's standards. Impos-
sibly late by the Mercantile Christmas Calendar, which
starts pumping "Jingle Bells" through the muzak pipes the
day after Halloween and sends truckloads of commercial
trees thundering south to Boston and New York before
Thanksgiving.

But here in upcountry Maine the quantity and year-
round availability of Christmas trees makes us pretty re-
laxed about hauling one home to put up in the living
room. I don't know how many balsam fir there are on our
hundred-and-some acres of woodlot, but I do know we
have enough. No need to race the crowds.

So even though we are behind the times, we still sleep a little later this morning than we do on work-and-school days, take our time with breakfast, make the Saturday-morning dump and post-office run, pour a third cup of coffee to sip while we read the mail and the paper. By the time I'm ready to go out scouting for a tree, the sun has clawed its way almost as far above the southern horizon as it cares to go at the winter solstice. It may be making a bright and smiling face this morning, but it's too far away to be sharing much heat with us, and the thermometer on the porch still hasn't climbed above 10 degrees. I pull on my Bean boots, an extra layer of wool, my choppers, and pick up the felling axe from the wood room.

To go into the woods encumbered by nothing more than an axe is a treat in itself. I usually cut my firewood in November and December, and it's rare that I go out onto the woodlot at this time of year without a lot of paraphernalia: ancient crawler tractor, chain saw, gas, bar oil, wedges, peavey, logging chain. Rattling and clanking is how I usually go, weighed down like Marley's ghost with the shackles of my labors. But this morning I feel light and agile as a chickadee. I too can flit from fir to spruce to naked maple, weaving my way through the lacework of shadows the sun casts on the snow.

Greg has come with me. He is seventeen now, but he is neither so blasé nor cool that he has given up this annual ritual we have shared since his early childhood. The selection of a Christmas tree may not be a matter of world-shaking importance, but it is important enough that no one should have to bear the responsibility of it alone.

There are five or six inches of snow on the ground,

enough to make it officially winter but not enough to make us don snowshoes; and before we have gone a hundred yards into the woods on the twitch road, we have veered off it and begun that wandering, rambling process of looking for the tree we want, comparing, reflecting, appraising. We do not, of course, move quite like chickadees. Earthbound, we have to push through the brush, leave tracks in the snow. But if we are not birdlike, we are at least animal-like, foraging and browsing, like deer or snowshoe hares, our tracks circling, looping, crisscrossing as we move from tree to tree, stopping here and there to do a little visual nibbling.

"This one's nice and full and just about the right height," I say.

"Too wimpy at the top," Greg says.

"We could cut that spiky tip off."

Greg will have none of that. It's fair to lop off a branch that's too long, but decapitation won't do. You can't ask an angel or the star of Bethlehem to sit on top of a headless tree. Neither of us is entirely clear about why that is so, but because the point seems self-evident to us both, we move on.

The next candidate looks perfect. It's on the edge of a small clearing, and in its uncrowded surroundings it has grown into a beautifully tapered yet bushy tree about eight feet tall. No argument about this one. But as I step in close to cut it, I see that it is really not a whole tree but only half a tree. Its contemporaries snuggled in behind it have shaded out the back of it entirely, and what is lush growth on its front is a mere skeleton in back. We have before us a false-front Christmas tree, like a storefront in a western.

We've been out for an hour or so by now, and with our feet starting to get cold we try a dodge we've tried before and should know better than ever to try again. We spot a fir about twenty-five feet tall, its crown free and clear above its neighbors. No crowding here. No lopsided growth. This baby is full and round and furry. We'll just drop it and take the top six or seven feet out of it.

But once we have it down, we realize that to get the gorgeously shaped and proportioned tree that we want and that we in fact saw from the ground, we'll have to take twelve feet, not six or seven. Our ceiling is eight feet high. Twelve will not do, and when we've cut our top down to room size and stand back to take a look at it, Greg says, again, "Too wimpy at the top."

Too wimpy farther down, too, as far as I'm concerned. What looked utterly grand up there against the blue of the winter sky is a pathetic fragment now that it has been slashed down to room size. To soothe my conscience about slaughtering this tree for naught, I limb the trunk out. When it's dry, I'll saw it up for summer wood.

We search some more. The woods are impressing on us once again the lesson they have taught us year after year: Nature abhors the perfect Christmas tree, and—now that I think about it—so do I. What ever made me think I wanted one of those flawlessly symmetrical cone-shaped things in the first place? The perfect Christmas tree is a horticultural artifact, an artifice, a hoax, a put-up job, a plantation product bred of pesticides, herbicides, fertilizers, and years of artful shearing and clipping that would put a prize Poodle to shame. It is an example of man trying to make nature imitate industry, a design taken from a

159

solid-geometry textbook and infinitely reproduceable in plastic; it's life in Lego Land.

On our woodlot, by contrast, our trees are shaped by the vagaries of shade, sun, and wind; of ice storms and sodden snows; of aphids and mites; of drought and deluge; of the thousand natural shocks that trees are heir to. It is those incalculable forces that account for all our lopsided, snaggletoothed, brown-needled, potbellied, wimpy-topped firs and spruce, trees that invite us to spend a few hours browsing among them, looking closely at their endless variety and eccentricity, enjoying the ones we leave every bit as much as—if not more than—the one we take home.

The tree we finally select is probably just as imperfect as many we have passed by, but we head home contented because it is not perfection we are celebrating. The pagan Teutonic tribes that orginated the custom of decorating their homes with evergreen trees at solstice time were not celebrating perfection either. They were celebrating the rolling around of the great celestial wheel, the turning point in the solar calendar that promised the greening of the earth and the rekindling of the hearth in the sky. They were celebrating benign forces that were both beyond them and that sustained them, and so they—like Greg and me—were happy to go out in the woods and make do with whatever trees they found there.

Country Singing

I'm struck time and again by the power group singing has over me, not singing I am audience to, but singing I take part in, singing that is, I suppose, not very "good" from a musical point of view. It's the singing you do in churches or at the end of the high school Christmas concert when the audience is invited to sing along, and it just plain bowls me over.

When it starts, I make a firm resolve that this time I will not be a sentimental old fool. This time I will sing "Rock of Ages" or "We Shall Overcome" or "O Little Town of Bethlehem" just like any other solid citizen—dry-eyed, full-voiced, no nonsense.

But resolves be damned. After a few bars, the tears are

about to leak down my face; the lump in my throat swells to watermelon proportions, and because it is difficult to sing around a watermelon, my otherwise unexceptional baritone begins to squeak, then gives out altogether.

The song does without me while a stern inner voice says, "Stop your blubbering. You're an embarrassment to us all."

"Oh, I know," I say, "I (sob!) know."

I get hold of myself and climb back onto the flow of song: "The hopes and fears of all the years . . ." But before I've made it through "are met in thee tonight," I've wiped out again.

It *is* an embarrassment, and I often wonder how many people have gone home from musical events in Farmington, Maine, and told their wives or husbands, "Gee, you know, I sat next to this guy at the concert tonight who cried all the way through 'Rudolf the Red-Nosed Reindeer.'"

I also wonder how many other closet weepers there are out there in the singing public. For years I've been asking myself that question, and for years I've been coming up with the same answer: "None, you maudlin sap."

Then just this past Christmas, after the community chorus concert, I was talking to a guy who is a superb violinist, a violin maker, a musician of the finest sensibility, in short, a man in whose musical judgment and instincts I put the utmost faith. After we had exchanged a few remarks about the afternoon's performance, he said to me: "But you know what just bowls me over? It's when everybody sings at the end. That whole auditorium full of people—all those voices, not trained singers or anything but just people singing—it chokes me up like nothing else I know."

"Sob sister," I said. "Aren't you ashamed?"

And then I fessed up.

I don't mean to claim any special powers for country singers and country singing. There are plenty of people living in cities who will know what I mean when I talk about that almost palpable blow to the midsection I feel when the voices of "my" people begin to sing, people I have lived with, against, and alongside of for years, people I'm fond of and not so fond of, people I positively can't stand today but may admire tomorrow, people I seek out and people I studiously avoid, all the people who are the color and fabric of this place that is my place in the world. As the Shaker hymn says, "'Tis a gift to come down where we ought to be." For some, that may be an urban neighborhood. For me, it's this patchwork of fields, ponds, forests, and hamlets in the foothills of the White Mountains, and singing began to assume the place it has in my life only after my wife and I made our permanent home here many years ago.

In our first winter we found ourselves part of a group of about a dozen people who met on Sunday afternoons to sing and play recorder together. We were all relative newcomers, all "from away," and the music we made together had a community-building effect, the kind it has for all immigrant groups that still have more in common with where they came from than with where they are. Our musical leader was Eric Leeber, a transplant from New

York City, who, with a Renaissance-music consort he called The Red House Circus, brought some wonderful evenings of music to western Maine.

It was an article of faith for Eric that audiences were not at concerts just to sit and gawk and listen, but to participate, too, and every Red House Circus concert included a lot of audience singing, mostly of rounds, which Eric loved to get rolling through an auditorium in eight parts. Those rounds would gather in the distance like a summer thunderstorm, slowly building to their full power as each new voice came in. Then, after one voice after another had dropped out again and the storm passed away down the valley, we would be left sitting there in the clean, fresh silence, the air positively dripping with the music you hear when the music stops. And Eric would grin and look around and nod his head and say, "Yeah, yeah."

When I was still a teenager, there was a French singing group that called itself *Les Compagnons de la Chanson*. I grant you it's a tacky name, both to the mind and the ear, but it suggests something of the companionability of songs and of the power of singing to make and maintain society, a power that came home to me recently on a wilderness canoe trip in Labrador. The singing our party did almost every night around the campfire was a ritual celebration of our small human community of nine where we were the only community there was, but it was also a celebration of our membership in the families and communities we had left behind and to which we would return. The singing was like the river itself. It was not something we "did." It was there, constantly flowing along; and in the evening, we would launch ourselves onto it, just as we set out on the river in the morning. It was a link to our past, both personal and communal, and it was a link to our future. It carried us out, and it would carry us back. It was both line and circle.

But for all the delights and illuminations that have come my way in singing with family, friends, and fellow way-farers, that small, closed-circle context is not the one in which singing affects me so powerfully that I sometimes wonder if my mental and emotional underpinnings are not giving way altogether. The essential condition for that experience is a large group that includes your whole local world, not just the people you invite to your house for dinner or the ones who invite you to theirs.

As for the singing itself, it is unrehearsed, ragged, far from perfect. People are off key. The back of the room may be lagging a bit behind the front, but still, it all works. There is an audible unity of purpose, and the voices that may not be doing just what they ought to do are heard as impromptu embellishments rather than unwanted distur-bances. The able singers who are the soloists and stars of church choirs, operettas, and close-harmony groups con-tinue to stand out here too, not alone, but as bright threads in the fabric, their voices blending in with everyone else's; and voices that are rarely or never heard in other circum-stances, the ones that are too shy to speak up at town meetings or in public debates, are in full voice.

It doesn't matter if one of us stumbles or even falls silent for a few bars. I can choke up as much as I want. The singing goes on, and the stumbler is carried along with it. Here the halt and the lame are not halt or lame at all. No one has to be persuasive, knowledgeable, coherent. There is no budget to be approved or cut, nobody on your side and nobody on my side. Perhaps the greatest miracle about a hall full of people singing is that we all speak and we all listen at the same time. Faces soften. Scrooges are transformed. We are not performing; rather, we are celebrating what we could perhaps be if we would only let ourselves. When we sing, we all become citizens of Utopia, of the Kingdom of God, call it what you will. When we walk out the door, we'll still be up against the same old stuff we're always up against; but for now and for as long as the singing lasts, we can hear clearly where it is we want to go, and every time I hear that song, it chokes me up like nothing else I know.

ABOUT THE AUTHOR

Robert Kimber's work has appeared in *Audubon, Country Journal, Down East, Field & Stream, Harrowsmith, Horticulture,* and *Yankee.* He is the author of the books, *A Canoeist's Sketchbook, Made for the Country,* and *Living Wild and Domestic: The Education of a Hunter-Gardener.* Kimber and his wife, Rita, have collaborated on upward of forty translations of books from the German, among them *Hannah Arendt, Karl Jaspers: Correspondence 1926–1969,* and *Anne Frank: The Biography.* The Kimbers live on an old farm in Temple, Maine.